TH
WEDDING GIFT

Waking Up Together

MARY & AUSTIN HENNESSEY

The Ultimate Guide for Successful Relationships

Note for Librarians: a cataloguing record for this book that includes Dewey Decimal Classification and US Library of Congress numbers is available from the Library and Archives of Canada. The complete cataloguing record can be obtained from their online database at:
www.collectionscanada.ca/amicus/indexe.html
ISBN 14120-3777-8
The examples of couples cited in this book are real; the names and circumstances have been changed to protect their anonymity and confidentiality.
Printed in Victoria, BC, Canada

TRAFFORD

Offices in Canada, USA, Ireland, UK and Spain
This book was published ondemand in cooperation with Trafford Publishing. Ondemand publishing is a unique process and service of making a book available for retail sale to the public taking advantage of ondemand manufacturing and Internet marketing. Ondemand publishing includes promotions, retail sales, manufacturing, order fulfilment, accounting and collecting royalties on behalf of the author.
Book sales for North America and international:
Trafford Publishing, 6E–2333 Government St.,
Victoria, BC v8t 4p4 CANADA
phone 250 383 6864 (tollfree 1 888 232 4444)
fax 250 383 6804; email to orders@trafford.com
Book sales in Europe:
Trafford Publishing (uk) Ltd., Enterprise House, Wistaston Road Business Centre, Wistaston Road, Crewe, Cheshire cw2 7rp United Kingdom
phone 01270 251 396 (local rate 0845 230 9601)
facsimile 01270 254 983; orders.uk@trafford.com
Order online at:
www.trafford.com/robots/04-1565.html

10 9 8 7 6 5 4 3 2

DEDICATION

This book is dedicated with boundless love and
gratitude to our daughter Jacinta whose
unwavering love and fierce loyalty are only
enhanced by her generosity of spirit.

From the moment you knocked on the door of
our hearts, we knew you were a gift from
heaven.

TABLE OF CONTENTS

ACKNOWLEDGMENTS

This book is a culmination of forty years of shared living, loving and learning. There are many visionaries and teachers who have had a profound influence on our thinking. Some of these special individuals helped stretch our thinking, woke us up, to such a degree that they irreversibly changed our perceptions of ourselves, the nature of the human experience, and the universe we live in. By helping us and others to appreciate the limitless boundaries of human and spiritual transformation (especially with regard to love), these seers have helped to pave the way before us. Their names are mentioned in the preface. To them we owe our heartfelt gratitude.

We wish to thank our parents, our first teachers of love. They set us on the path and have since gone to other dimensions to further explore the mysteries of love.

We especially appreciate our daughter Jacinta and son-in-law Daniel whose immense support and sense of humor have lifted our spirits through the tough times and who have wholeheartedly shared in our joys. Their belief in, and enthusiasm for this project inspired us to stay on focus.

Mary expresses her love and gratitude to her soul sister, Brigid, for the journey of love and healing they have shared together and for her unwavering support for our work.

ACKNOWLEDGMENTS

To Mia Lupton at Millennia Graphics, we thank her for a magnificent job with the cover and layout. Her esthetic sense interpreted our fledgling ideas beautifully, and through it all she was both patient and gracious.

No book would ever see the light of day without a skilled editor. Our heartfelt thanks go to our editor Ann Westlake for being gentle and incisive, encouraging and timely.

We are deeply grateful to Bruce Batchelor for his insight in establishing Trafford Publishing. His courage and ingenuity are a gift to writers. We are indebted to Angela Aidoo, publishing consultant, for her gentle persistence and for the many ways she has facilitated our initiation into the world of publishing. To all the staff at Trafford, thank you for transforming this manuscript into book form.

We will be forever grateful to our many friends who have steadfastly believed in us and supported our work. They include: Pascal and Cathie Menezes, Dave and Louise Inchauspe, Dave and Liz Krise, Karin and Daniel Lannigan, Nancy Frasu, Chris Saladen and Gary Edighoffer, Don and Donna Rockstrom, Chavanna King, Michael and Mary Maughan, Larry and Katherine Sandrin, Lynda Mackie, Richard and Nancy Mackie, Jo-Anne Evans, Rob Barrett and Diana McFarlane, Les & Annabelle Trask, and Gordon Bryenton. Mark Mays and Al Turtle deserve our sincere gratitude for sharing their clarity and wisdom.

To all those who attend our lectures, we extend our sincere appreciation. They consistently afford us the opportunity to share the vital message of authentic living.

To the many couples who have shared their lives and loves with us, we treasure their dreams and aspirations for a deeper experience of heartfelt relationship. We thank them for trusting the ideas expressed in this book and for proving their effectiveness. We are extremely grateful for their enthusiasm and feedback.

In conclusion, we thank you for letting us share with you the life-changing message of awakened relationships. May each of us awaken from our spiritual sleep and become conscious of our precious relationship with each other and with Life.

A LOVER'S INVITATION

Come, my beloved, and let's agree, you and I, that the societal conventions of guarded hearts, tight-reined emotions, swallowed words, and the need to be right, or perfect, can be waived between our hearts.

I want to experience this freedom with at least one other person – and that person is you. Can you agree to suspend the hardness and rigidity of society's expectations and come play with me in the garden of love's fullness?

What would you bring to that garden, my love? Bring your playful self; the part of you that likes to frolic, laugh and have fun; that part of you that can drop convention as naturally as you dropped yesterday's clothes. Leave your mask of expectation and pretense behind and show yourself to me in all your splendor. And I will do the same for you.

Together, let us explore other worlds, where intimate togetherness consumes us, where time is suspended so we can do everything we've ever dreamed we would. Satiated with love's unrestricted bounty, we embrace each other purely as love's gift. Come with me and let's drink from love's delectable well of openness, truth and unmitigated trust. For here we are free of pretense, striving, resistance, hiding and bewilderment.

Come now and laugh in wondrous joy and marvel at love's expansiveness. So much more to see and experience; rejoice, my beloved, and know that here you are safe and secure from the ravages of love's afflictions. Your heart needs no armor, no moats or walls, for you are protected by your own strength and loveliness. In this chamber of shared love we can discover the strength of vulnerability, the pure forgiveness of yesterday's follies and the open embrace of love's promises.

Come, my precious love, and dare to soar above what the world offers as romantic love. Come and probe the depths of fantasy – you and me and the eternal floating in a sea of fathomless joy. Come away, my beloved, to taste those exquisite moments of enchantment where only you and I, together, can penetrate love's mystery and return renewed, refreshed and transformed. For that is the essence of love's gift, to give itself without reservation or conditions, without containment or restriction. It alone knows its expansive nature and waits patiently for us to surrender to its ineffable secrets.

Together, let us take flight, rise above the mundane and the ordinary, and bask in the sensation of delight reserved for those who willingly risk spreading their wings so they can rendezvous in the pleasant warmth of the heart, and sip love's nectar from the cup of bliss.

PREFACE

I think a man and a woman should choose each other for life, for the simple reason that a long life with all its accidents is barely enough time for a man and a woman to understand each other and... To understand – is to love.

WILLIAM BUTLER YEATS

Falling in love can be one of the most exhilarating experiences of being human. Poets and dramatists have, for centuries, romanticized and immortalized this most exquisite of all human encounters. It is indeed a magical moment when we discover the joy of deep, passionate romance with our lover. This inexplicable, irrational and irresistible attachment to another defies logic and is best described as a mystery of the heart. This twinning of hearts in intimate relationship provides the key to unraveling love's mysteries. Only in the shelter of a loving heart can we experience the breadth and depth, the beauty and enchantment of love's most precious treasures.

When we, the authors, were stricken with Cupid's arrow we wanted a relationship of equality, and shared togetherness. So we started out by examining existing relationship theories and putting research under close scrutiny in the laboratory of our daily life together. Fortunately, we shared a fascination for psychology, specifically the psychology of loving.

We chose this particular path because, from the very beginning, our perspective on relationship was anchored in the shared acceptance that marriage was a sacred contract. From that premise, we set out to discover, for ourselves, how we could honor that agreement while staying romantic lovers, raising a family and becoming, what the American psychologist, Abraham Maslow, called "self-actualized". We dreamed that somehow we'd enjoy the perfect soul mate relationship and together discover our life purpose. In short, we wanted it all! And we were too young and idealistic to think we couldn't have it all!

Why, you wonder, did we have such far-reaching goals? Before we met, Austin had spent several years in a seminary training to be a priest. Mary had spent some years in a convent studying to be a nun. When we met, the magnetic attraction was so powerful it was love at first sight. Since neither of us had much romantic experience, we decided we'd grow and learn together.

The minute I heard my first love story, I started looking for you,
not knowing how blind that was. Lovers don't finally meet somewhere.
They're in each other all along.
MAULANA JALALU'DDIN RUMI

It would be easy to say that the gods have smiled on us. But we know only too well that relationship means more than heavenly benedictions and flights of fantasy (although these are amazingly pleasurable interludes). Through experience, we've learned that successful marriage is an affair of the heart, rooted in common sense and daily attention to thoughts and feelings, and the behaviors and attitudes that flow from them. We discovered that love, the heart of successful relationship, can be strong and vulnerable, playful and serious, open and closed, wounded and forgiving, and through it all remain the rock, the safety net, the inspiration, and the attracting force that keeps us connected.

Our history and experience have taught us that love is the gift we continuously give to each other: the knowing smile, the unspoken words, the flirting glance, the tender touch, the warm embrace, the enchanting kiss. Love is the gift of waking up together, sharing the positive energy that makes the heart sing and opens the deepest recesses of our souls to the mirrored reflection of our true self.

Throughout these many years together, our love continues to mature and our dreams, one by one, are becoming reality. While raising a family and attending to the unfolding of our careers, we've had ample opportunities to test the boundaries and depths of love as we moved through the inevitable challenges of work and raising children.

Our careers came full circle when we felt the urge again to dedicate our lives to helping others. We completed our spiritual and psychological training and launched into our new work of lecturing to groups and mentoring couples to more effective living. Since then, our lives have been an accelerated school for personal transformation.

As counselors and relationship mentors, we've had the opportunity to see the human condition in its many forms. People from all socio-economic levels knocked on our doors; some were desperate, some were searching and many were bewildered. The story was always the same – with slight variations. They had come face-to-face with their own humanness and felt ill-equipped to fathom its depths. From their hearts they poured out chronicles of loss and pain, fear and suffering. For some, the problem was financially rooted; others despaired about their errant sons and daughters, aging parents or loss of employment. But most of them were concerned with the complexities of relationship; love lost, love denied, love cheated, love misunderstood, love betrayed, loneliness, emptiness, regret and remorse for what might have been. Some easily expressed their hurt. Others remained numb, angry or fearful, in search of any comfort or compassion that might rejuvenate a heart closed and shrunken by the excruciating pain of love's disillusionment.

Most of these folks were simply traveling love's path and had lost their way. Some claimed they never had a map to direct them through the maze of love's intricacies. Others asked for guidance on the best roads, milestones or signposts, and avoidable detours in the uncharted territory of the heart.

In response to this apparent void in relationship know-how, we offered mentoring programs for couples. Our intention was to provide a road map for those embarking on committed relationships and to fill a need for those who had run into roadblocks and, in their disillusionment, had thought of giving up. The criteria for enrollment were very clear; either they were starting out and wanted help in charting their course or they were in committed relationships and needed input in order to enhance the experience. Couples wanted to know the secrets or magic that permeated our togetherness. Pretty soon there were no secrets. Every session was magic-filled as we shared our own heartfelt experiences. The sessions were conducted in an environment of love and acceptance and were successful beyond our wildest imagining.

Following a visit to Paris, France, our work took on a new sense of contribution. We were particularly inspired during a visit to Père LaChaise cemetery and the mausoleum erected in honor of Abélard and Héloïse, the most celebrated romantic lovers of the Middle Ages. The fact that their relationship took place so long ago only adds to its sentimental appeal. Abélard was the most renowned teacher of his day, handsome and brilliant, she, his attractive, well-bred intellectual student and the recipient of his amorous advances. Both deserve to be immortalized as examples of 'courtly love' (the affinity of two souls for a noble purpose) and precursors of the more modern paradigm of committed relationship. Like all couples in love, they had their problems. Although the church had allowed clerics to marry, opinion was changing and Abélard felt the authorities would view his career as a teacher of philosophy and theology incompatible with the status of marriage.

Love, however, could not be denied, so the couple resolved their dilemma by secretly affirming their marriage vows. When their secret became public, Héloïse's family was outraged and vengefully punished her new husband. She took refuge in a convent, he in a monastery, and each continued to vow unending love for the other. In spite of the fact that they were now forced to live apart, a love affair of the heart and soul continued throughout their lives, as evidenced in their exchange of love letters. True love always finds a way, and although they could not be reunited in their mortal lives, they were eventually entombed together.

I love thee, I love but thee with a love that shall not die
till the sun grows cold and the stars grow old.
WILLIAM SHAKESPEARE

Their final resting place has become a celebrated shrine to the power, beauty and steadfastness of love. It is frequented by lovers of all ages bearing red roses. They come to lay their floral tributes at the tomb of love's immortal presence and silently pray that such a meaningful union of heart, soul and mind might bless their own togetherness.

It was a balmy June afternoon, while on our own pilgrimage to the lovers' shrine, that our lives were again deeply touched by love's magic. We were emotionally moved as we stood in the accumulated energy of 900 years of love's promises declared, renewed and heartfully expressed. In that moment, we became acutely aware of the need in our world for more advocacy for the beauty and power of romantic, intimate, authentic love. As we tenderly placed our roses at the foot of the lovers' resting place, we committed to make a contribution by sharing, in writing, our perceptions and experiences of love's journey. For us, that journey is about rediscovering the heart of intimate relationship. It's about knowing and honoring ourselves and each other, being both teachers and students of life and love.

Our research, just like our journey, is eclectic. We have been blessed with a series of teachers who have inspired us; some were gentle, soothing and caring, while others were disturbing and demanding in their attempts to wake us up! For teaching us the transforming power of love, these teachers deserve special recognition. Their gifts are often invisible, yet gracious and uplifting. We have come often to drink at the well of Marianne Williamson, Harville Hendrix, Evelyn and Paul Moschetta, Gay and Kathlyn Hendricks, Susan Campbell, Howard and Charlotte Clinebell, Erich Fromm, and others.

Some teachers have the special gift of opening the vaults of hearts and exposing their treasures. We especially appreciate the flow of love from the hearts of John O'Donohue, Paula Reeves, Leo Buscaglia, Frank Andrews and the many other hearts whose mission it is to bring more love into a world that hungers for its warmth.

Our egos recoiled in the presence of Jack Boland who insisted that we admit our goofiness and transform it. He introduced us to the teachings of George Gurdjieff, a practical mystic, and the Russian philosopher P.D. Ouspensky. These seers believed passionately in the evolution of human consciousness. Their ideas were further expanded and explained in the works of Maurice Nicholl and Vernon Howard, teachers of amazing brilliance and insight. Their spiritual/psychological approach is reduced to the simplest terms for all to understand. With the conviction and rigor of any Zen master they instruct us to see life as a practical experiment in getting to know ourselves. They remind us why we need to discover the reasons that our lives are so often at odds with our best intentions – and go to work to transform them!

Practice self-observation (know thyself), they insisted. Honest soul-searching and rigorous confrontation of our egos is an ongoing pursuit. With even a small effort we began to get insight into the concept that we are only prisoners of our own 'not knowing'. Our self-knowledge expanded exponentially when we were introduced to the masterful precision of Guy Finley whose prodigious work in the Gurdjieffian tradition is uncompromising and laser-like. We also thank Byron Katie for her distilling synthesis of the workings of the inner self, our ability to confront our perceptions, discover the truth and free ourselves from our 'story' into the fullness of life. Under these teachers' tutelage, our lives have literally been transformed. We owe them a debt of gratitude.

Ken Wilber, Andrew Cohen and others have brought home to us

the urgent imperative of conscious evolution and our calling to participate in it. This, we now appreciate, is the self-realization advocated by Abraham Maslow. Again the message is simple: learn to truly know yourself and others and relate more compassionately to the world around you. Reach for a global vision and find your place in it. Some of those teachers who have affected our lives in a profound way, include: Wayne Dyer, Deepak Chopra, Joan Borysenko, Marsha Sinetar, Michael Lerner, Louise Hay, Jean Vanier, Neale Donald Walsch, Elizabeth Lesser and Jacquelyn Small. They all carry a compelling message: turn within and discover the true meaning of life. You can live a purposeful life even in the chaos of our materialistic, egocentric world. Thank you for this enlightened view of life – we continue to nourish ourselves from your rich teachings.

It is a glorious moment when one knows, at the deepest place within one's self, the truth of Einstein's own discovery: everyday the voice of God speaks to us and we decide whether the universe is a benevolent or a malevolent place. We simply take responsibility for our choices and their outcomes. How freeing! No more judgment. No more blame. Each is in charge of his/her own world. How comforting!

The luminaries of soul are a provocative presence in a world that has forgotten its true identity. Their clarion call rings loud and clear as it summons us into a deeper, richer, stronger understanding of the mystery of our own being. Our souls reverberate with a song of gratitude to Meister Eckhart, Gary Zukav, Richard Bucke, Harry Moody, St. Theresa of Lisieux, Christian Larson, Walter Starcke, John Randolph Price, Joel Goldsmith, Neville Goddard, Emmet Fox, Eric Butterworth, Marcus Bach, John Sanford and the numerous others who have worked quietly for a better world.

As part of our own spiritual path, we have been influenced by the wisdom expressed in the writings of Norman Vincent Peale, Richard Bach, Stuart Wilde, Shakti Gawain, Alan Cohen, Robin Casarjian, Jon Kabat-Zinn, Thich Nhat Hanh, Daniel Goleman, Shad Helmstetter, Carolyn Myss, Jean Houston, Barbara Marx Hubbard, John Shelby Spong, and the unnamed ones who have so blended with our own psyches that we can never forget them.

These are the many streams that flow into the river we call the journey of our life together.

The story of love inspired by the medieval lovers Abélard and Héloïse is tightly woven into the fabric of our own hearts. In the context of their spiritual calling, their hearts were inseparable even though they could no longer enjoy the warmth of each other's presence. We feel immensely blessed that our souls, hearts, and life purpose have all converged in an exhilarating life of shared love and growth.

We felt moved to write this book as a testament to the power of love that can evoke romance, pleasure, awe, mystery and adventure. It is love that lifts our hearts, souls and minds to the highest frontiers of satisfied living. To that end, we invite you to look deeper into your own heart and mind and become the observer of your thoughts and feelings as you continue to search for the ultimate goal of happiness, fulfillment, growth and joy in your mutual love. Because it is difficult for any of us to be truly objective about ourselves, the clearest way to see ourselves is through the eyes of another. The path of relationship affords us the best opportunity to learn and evolve together. This learning may require soul-searching so as to honestly confront our ego or false self, and be willing to let go of our old 'stories' as to how life, and love should be, and embrace the reality of what is. The willingness to transform our past and create our future together invites a whole new dimension of depth, warmth, and purpose to our married relationship.

During our lectures, we could not reach every couple individually. Consequently, many of them sought us out for private mentoring. The principles expressed in this book have helped hundreds of couples wake up and regain their footing on the road to informed and empowered relationship. Many hundreds more have discovered the missing pieces that enabled them to return to the bliss they once enjoyed and thought they had lost forever.

We make no claim to be experts on marriage – for who can claim to be expert on the human experience? Our intent is to share perceptions that hopefully shed light on the journey of shared togetherness.

INTRODUCTION

This book is right for you ...

If you've just become engaged and want to know how to create the type of marriage that is romantic, adventurous, fully alive and happy...

If you've had an idyllic wedding and honeymoon and you long to remain intimately attracted and deeply involved with your spouse over the long term...

If you are successful in other areas of your life but find it difficult to maintain a loving relationship...

If you are open to the idea that waking up in relationship means becoming more conscious (aware) of your relationship with life, yourself, and your partner...

If you are curious about the deeper reason that drew you to your spouse and are willing to explore the evolving ideal of authentic living.

Why are so many couples disappointed in love? They fall in love so easily but have trouble staying there. Somehow the magic slips away, leaving them confused and empty. Well-meaning friends try to comfort them by suggesting that maybe it wasn't meant to be, or that what they felt was just a fleeting glimpse into real love. But their hearts know better. Yes, their hearts truly did take flight to enchanted places; they've been to the moon and tasted its ecstasy and don't ever want to forget. But in the sobering light of day, the romantic excursions feel barren and lifeless. And the nagging question remains: "How can I hold on to this love?"

Many look to psychology for answers to their painful disappointments and broken dreams. But psychology doesn't have the answers. Even though the word psychology literally means "soul knowledge", it is devoid of soul and focuses instead on matters related to the personality. And here we have the crux of the problem. Too many of us are preoccupied with our own needs and wants. Our constant search for adventure, meaning and love in a three dimensional world that rewards greed and materialism, becomes a narcissistic indulgence in the demands of our personality. The only way to end this self-centered relationship with life and love is to recognize and move beyond the separate ego that perpetuates it. It is this waking up to the truth of what is driving our life and relationships that frees us from the prison of our personality into the aliveness of being fully human. This is the beginning of authentic living.

Some look directly to spirituality for the answer to their sense of loneliness and lack of meaning. They are searching for a connection to something larger than the current experience of their contracted human self. Innate in the human spirit is the urge to overcome the false understanding that sees us as separate, lost and alone, with no higher purpose than to look out for ourselves. This invisible crisis of meaning can only be resolved through reconnecting with our inner selves and the loving capacities that reside there. We call this spirituality.

Spirituality is a new way of seeing –ourselves and our world– and a new way of being. Spirituality is not religion, although the original purpose of religion was to guide us to realizing our full capacity as spiritual beings. Alas, many feel their religion has failed them, and they continue to feel isolated and disconnected. A large number of us have discovered our spiritual selves in ways that are independent of any religion. Discovering our spirituality means embracing the realm of ultimate freedom: freedom from our narrow sense of self (we are only human), freedom from attachment to the real or imagined pain of the past (our story), freedom to transcend the human tendency to project unto others the pain that was imposed on us (breaking the repetitive cycle), freedom from living our lives according to the expectations of others (societal demands), freedom from the greed of our Western culture (pervasive materialism). This capacity for freedom and transcendence, this ability to know ourselves in a larger context is what we call soul. To the degree that we embrace our spiritual self, we express our soul.

In this book, we propose an emergent view of authentic relationship. Couples no longer need to form partnerships for economic survival as they did in the past; marriage, like everything else, evolves over time. Today's couples yearn for heartfelt belonging, honest mutual recognition, and soulful connection. They want to believe that romance and intimacy are possible, but many are afraid to risk vulnerability, and fear rejection. Take heart. The enchantment of romantic love is very much alive. Its evolution is charted in the journey of awakening that winds its way through the magic of attraction to the reality of honest soul-searching into the flowering of authentic living.

The notion that partners attract each other for the purpose of waking up together is just dawning above the horizon of our collective consciousness. Being awake means seeing life clearly – knowing what one stands for. When couples wake up together they realize more fully "I am *for* you – I am here to support you becoming all you are capable of being and I am receptive to your support for my awakening." Before we can be awake to each other we must first be awake to ourselves. Being awake is about becoming aware of our negative unconscious connections with those parts of ourselves that restrict our view of life and love.

The postmodern viewpoint is that as we confront the unresolved issues of our personality, our soul evolves itself and shifts to a higher level of consciousness. This is transformation. This is the process of waking up. This is the beginning of authentic living.

This expanded personal awareness facilitates the process of freeing us into a deeper relationship with each other and with life. This attraction of souls for the purpose of spiritual growth and personal transformation is the truest intent of the soul mate relationship. Richard Bach (author of numerous books including The Bridge Across Forever) describes soul mates in this way; "A soul mate is someone who has the locks to fit our keys, and the keys to fit our locks. When we feel safe enough to open the locks, our truest selves step out and we can be completely and honestly who we are; we can be loved for who we are and not for what we are pretending to be... Our soul mate is someone who shares our deepest longings, our sense of direction... Our soul mate is the one who makes life come to life."

The true soul mate relationship evolves over time; it takes shape as we move from emotional fluctuating states of love – what we call conditional love – to timeless, agape (spiritual) or unconditional love. It parallels the evolution in marriage from unconscious love (unaware, asleep) to conscious love (awake) to authentic living. Let us guide you on the journey to discovering your soul mate relationship and enjoy the exquisite nature of a satisfying and lasting love.

Our aim is to facilitate the waking up process. To that end we offer healthy, positive mentoring that assists couples to discover the deepest joy in relationship by helping them to identify what is most true about them. By this we mean becoming self aware and stepping up to a more authentic way of living; we also refer to it as self-realization. This mentoring, or transformational coaching, is a potent communication process that helps couples wake up to what is real in the "now moment." Embracing this reality frees us from the burdens of unconscious living and our attachment to painful past events. This mutual support for individual and couple growth is the path to spiritual or awakened partnership.

Our purpose in writing this book is to share what we have learned about awakened partnership and its capacity to transform relationship into authentic shared living that embraces the deepest levels of both intimacy and romance. Additionally, we intend to shed light on the postmodern context of marriage as a vehicle for personal transformation.

Marriage can be an accelerated path to personal and spiritual growth. No other relationship has quite the same power to transform lives. In The Best Possible Wedding Gift we will explore the nature of committed relationship, and we'll show how to evolve this shared togetherness into the partnership most couples dream of. We will mentor you in the heart-centered subtleties that create and sustain the love, passion and compassion that are the fuel of an awakened marriage. We will introduce practices that enable you to reduce the stresses that often hamper relationships. As you proceed through the ideas we share, we will guide you to ways you can discover, or rediscover, the celebration of trust, joy, play, commitment, and pleasure in your shared lives.

The tragedy of recent times is that so much preparation is given to the wedding day, and yet so little thought is given to a life of marriage. When we awaken to the full spectrum and variety of possibilities within marriage, and how these impact us, we have even more cause to celebrate. A sense of well-being evolves naturally when we focus on expanding our awareness of our self and our spouse, and especially when this is nurtured in an environment of heart-centered love and compassion.

This book can be used as a guide to fill any vacancies in your understanding or appreciation of love's nature. It will prepare you to embrace the mystery of love, entertain its changing nature with awareness and skill; bask in its joy, laughter and tears and share its sweet nectar with your lover. We will point out the markers and signposts others have graciously left along love's often unpredictable, but well-trodden path. We have attempted to gather together some notable beliefs, practices, and rituals of those lovers and spiritual travelers who have opened their hearts to love and refined for us the art of loving. Their legacy is priceless.

For the purpose of this book we define "marriage" as a coming together of two emotionally committed people, dedicated to each other's personal and spiritual growth in ways that create a deepened intimacy, where both partners feel deeply loved and fully valued. The information gathered here is of equal value to singles who may be contemplating a romantic partnership. Many of the ideas expressed may prove helpful to those who have walked love's path and been disappointed. Divorce is sometimes regarded as a failure; we prefer to treat it as a learning experience. Only the brave can risk being vulnerable again. Love waits.

You will notice that we sometimes refer to the partners as "he" or "she" without mentioning the opposite gender, although it applies. Our intention is to be inclusive.

In the first chapter, we will share why every couple answering the call of the heart to committed relationship needs to prepare for this life-transforming process we call marriage. We explain why both romance and struggle are predictable parts of the journey, and that the path to true growth and fulfilled dreams is one of working through these phases together.

In the second chapter, we explore effective ways for coping with some of our unconscious issues. Creating a conscious marriage involves reclaiming aspects of ourselves that have been repressed. In partnership, we can effectively help each other learn from our earlier life experiences by drawing on the healing energy of the heart to free ourselves into the fullness of love.

In chapter three, we discuss the importance of shared values. Values are the heart principles that permeate our togetherness and our individual lives. While we each have our core values, together, we select those principles that will guide and direct our behaviors and decisions as a couple.

The fourth chapter introduces the power of imagination as we come together to create a vision for marriage. This is an opportunity to bring intention to our deepest hopes and dreams for the life we are creating together. When we collaborate on a clear, common vision, our relationship has greater meaning and a depth of focus that will attract the desired fulfillment.

Chapter five addresses the awareness of emotional nurturing. One of the markers along the path of conscious loving is the awareness that many of the difficulties that arise in marriage are signals that some need of one or both partners is not being nurtured. When we are willing to engage the compassion of the heart and soothe the emotions of our lover, we enjoy a relationship filled with contentment and happiness.

Chapter six exposes how clear, open communication promotes growth, healing, closeness, and builds a reservoir of emotional energy that can be tapped for problem solving and conflict resolution. Communication, the mutual exchange of both thoughts and feelings, expresses the language of the heart and is the cornerstone of a healthy relationship. The free flow of ideas clearly expressed within the couple relationship shapes the vitality of their togetherness.

Chapter seven recognizes and offers solutions to the added stresses of married life. Today, more couples are working and sharing domestic responsibilities, and feeling overwhelmed and stressed. Here we introduce effective ways to reduce and manage those stresses, and relax into the comfort of love's easy flow.

Chapter eight investigates one of the often contentious issues in relationship – money. An old adage says, 'When money is tight, couples fight.' This doesn't have to be true but it is easier to build a great relationship when money issues are handled effectively. In this chapter, we examine how the key to financial success for couples is financial knowledge and a practical appreciation of how money works.

In this ninth chapter, we look at ways to deepen sexual intimacy. In the intimate rendezvous of the heart, couples can experience their sensual selves in ways that embellish their love for each other. Here we discuss the value and necessity for open communication in sexual matters.

Chapter ten clarifies how the soul mate relationship, that honest reflection of one's self in the soul of another, is the greatest gift imaginable and the flowering of intimate connection. Lovers, whose hearts have found shelter and compassion in each other, discover the mysterious quality of enchantment that infuses their lives. As we walk the path of relationship together, our lives become a continual flow of welcome life-learning events.

Wherever you are on the relationship journey it is never too late to revisit the heart, revise the plan and drink from the well of love's hope and newness. You have all the essentials to create a loving relationship that will nurture your heart, lift your spirits and open you to the fullness of life in ways you rarely thought possible.

CHAPTER 1

Answering the Call of the Heart

⟵⟶

Everything that lives, lives not alone, nor for itself.

WILLIAM BLAKE

Mary's recollection: When I was a child, I was certain I would never marry. It gave me no joy in those growing years to see the raging discontent in my father's eyes. I never knew what ignited the fire of anger in him. Mother was different. Sometimes her face was confident and radiant as she attended to her household responsibilities while singing to her heart's content. But mostly a silent sadness hung around her. Tension and fear were her daily companions. John McGahern's novel Angry Women is a realistic portrayal of the dynamic of silent anger and fearful passivity that played out daily in our household. Every year or two a new baby arrived. Soon the small house was crowded and I felt lost, almost like I was no longer sure where I belonged. My parent's life together seemed heavy and burdensome and I wanted no part of such a fate!

The nuns at the parochial school appeared to be joyless women who, I now surmise, thrived on their authority to control large numbers of naive kids. Occasionally one of them would flash a beam of kindness in my direction and I'd savor it for weeks. I excelled at my class work because I wanted them to like me – maybe even praise me when I won the book prize for perfect attendance or the best report card. Winning the approval of adults at home or at school was important to me. I wanted to be loved, noticed, to feel that I belonged.

My grandfather was a charismatic person who inspired me. He ignited my sense of wonder, delight and a childlike belief in the inherent goodness of the world around me. He was a man at peace with himself notwithstanding his personal challenges. I wanted to be with him to savor his confidence, self-assurance, courage and love for the beauty of life itself.

From him I learned about the cycles in nature – he was involved in horticulture – and the ability of music to touch the soul. Together we made pilgrimages to the 'holy wells' (small shrines erected over shallow wells of healing water) in Irish country villages where we prayed for miracles. We sat around the fire at night and traded stories. When I told him that I was afraid of ghosts he took me to a haunted house and taught me that ghosts cannot harm us. He believed that these phantoms are only illusions; to him they represented invisible thought forms and shapes from our past. I didn't quite understand his point of view, but if he believed it, that was good enough for me. Above all else, my grandparents appeared to be genuinely fond of each other. I felt warm and comfortable in their presence. My visits with them were a treat because theirs was the one place where I felt a sense of belonging. It was many years before I felt that warmth and sense of belonging again.

The Universal Longing to Belong

The deepest longing in every human heart is the yearning to belong and to feel that our life has meaning. The sense of belonging or connectedness that you feel with your lover in the married relationship is the energy of your souls that called you to each other. Touched by love's magic, you believe that you were made for each other. Your inner world is so filled with contentment that no stress or ill wind could ruin this feeling of heaven on earth. This love you found is rich, deep, joyful, compassionate, selfless and unconditional. You are by now truly convinced that love must be the glue that holds the universe together. It embraces only good things and has magical powers. It has the power to dissolve anger and clear away resentment. It has the power to see deeply into another's burdened heart and find there the qualities that no one else can see.

As you begin your new life together, your hearts are filled with feelings of great possibilities for your relationship and you celebrate your happiness with your family and friends. The wedding and the honeymoon continue to reinforce the enchantment of your sense of oneness. Filled with hopes and dreams for your future together, you commit to sharing your lives forever! You feel a strong bond together even though you have not yet fully realized how your search for meaning is so intricately woven into your souls' finding each other. This is the beginning of your shared journey of exploration and discovery. The good news is that the magic of the love and romance you now feel can carry you through all the stages of your growth together if you are willing to become conscious in your relationship.

Should we expect the path of true love to be always smooth and trouble free? Many couples experience great difficulties in their relationship, often going their separate ways and claiming irreconcilable differences. Well-intentioned people who want deep and fulfilling relationships fail because they are unprepared and unable to cope with the problems that inevitably arise. Having no sense of personal intimacy, and unaware that their situation is the result of the choices they make, they take great pain to explain how their partner is the cause of their problem. Unconscious and unskilled, they go blindly to the next relationship and repeat the same pattern. Some suffer too much to want to stay in the search for love and finally surrender to loneliness or get involved in abusive relationships. Nothing seems to work the way they thought it should!

It is a significant moment when one realizes that the genesis of an intimate relationship is the ability to love oneself. Only when we love ourselves can we attract another into our circle of intimacy. While we hope that the function of marriage is to serve the facilitation of heartfelt belonging, it is a sad fact that many marriages never become truly intimate.

The real problem is that we lack understanding of the basic principles of living shared lives. These principles are available and waiting to nurture, comfort and assist us towards fulfilling our dream of a happy marriage. Absent this knowledge, couples are left vulnerable and subject to suffering, pain and the possible loss of their dreams for a life of bliss together.

We encourage you to consciously embrace the principles for loving and for creating a marriage filled with true intimacy. It is possible to experience the partnership of your dreams filled with love and bliss. We hope that you will not settle for a marriage of convenience, devoid of companionship or passion, but will use the principles we share to create your own special marriage filled with love and passion! The marriage you both dreamed of on your wedding day can be yours. Don't settle for anything less!

Falling in love is a deeply moving experience. It is the movement of the spirit of love within the hearts of two people, drawing them into a closer union that can only be fully realized with time and experience together.
WORDS FROM A MARRIAGE CEREMONY

Is Love Enough?

One of the societal myths about marriage is that either it works really well or it doesn't work at all. You either 'hit it off' or you're miserable. If the bloom of love fades, you can walk away and look for someone else to love. In our lectures on love and relationships we emphasize the importance of staying committed to the relationship. Couples feed back how much they appreciate this reminder. Deep down they believe they can build a life together. Often they are unsure how to apply their loving energy to make it happen, and yet they feel that it is their commitment that sustains them through the peaks and valleys of shared living.

The Beatles' song says, "*All You Need is Love*". Love can be a very inclusive term. Love opens the door to understanding. This understanding helps you to probe deeper into the nature of relationship, your partner and yourself. Too many couples go blindly into marriage lulled by the illusion that because they love each other so much, everything will automatically work out. Marriage itself is never a solution – it merely provides the vehicle that can transport us through the unraveling of love's complexities. Most of us have exaggerated and unrealistic expectations about shared togetherness. We are so romantically attached that we feel our closeness is sufficient to shield us from all our problems. Too often we are hypnotized into thinking that in the euphoria of such perfect love all our hurts will somehow be healed. Indeed they can be. We personally discovered that it takes work, discipline, patience and individual growth for this gift to become a reality.

Our ability to build intimacy with others is directly related to the bond of intimacy we have created with our 'self'. Intimacy, as we refer to it here, implies a deep understanding and appreciation of one's self. Opening up to the depth of our real self is a labor of love that cannot be contained in any framework of chronological time. No one can predict the duration of apprenticeship when it comes to the lessons of the heart.

As you settle into the often challenging process of intimate living, you will discover that your partnership is the ideal, though sometimes unwelcome, vehicle for your deeper self-understanding. Opportunities will arise daily that offer insights about values, qualities and emotional patterns. These insights inspire you to keep opening to each other and find shelter in each other's hearts. You begin to experience the comfort and safety of your shared lives and intimate love.

Embracing Change and Challenges

So what are the likely challenges you will face as you journey together? Someone said of marriage that it is "a dramatic act in which two people come together to find and redefine themselves." Marriage vows often include a promise about staying together until death do us part. They usually don't ask us to promise to stay the same throughout the relationship. Yet we resist change as though it were neither wanted nor needed.

Sometimes your dreams will seem to fall apart,
all kinds of things will get in the way, you will encounter many
roadblocks. Just don't let them stop you in your tracks.
See them simply as opportunities to grow through to the next level of life
together. Just commit to persist and you will achieve your desires.

CALVIN COOLIDGE

Marriage can be a real eye-opener! One of its consistent lessons is that living together involves continuous change and the overcoming of diverse challenges. The variety of problems confronted and fully experienced is part of life's journey whether alone or with a partner. These life experiences serve to enhance the growth of our lives individually and together; we could consider them opportunities for mastering life. The afterglow of rising above life's fray leaves us strong in mind, happy in heart and energetically revitalized. Additionally, working together to find solutions builds mutual confidence and trust.

Over time, aspects of each other's personalities previously hidden from view in the dizzy haze of passionate romantic love will begin to appear. Your call is to be alert to what appears like obstacles in your relationship, and to move mindfully through this maze of previously uncharted territory. Skillful handling of these surprise detours provides the building blocks for laying the path towards what Abraham Maslow called 'self-actualization.'

Early in our relationship, we were influenced by Maslow's

concept of an ongoing realization of one's potential, capacities and talents as fulfillment of a call to a more integrated life. His theories held enormous appeal and supplied spiritual nourishment for our journey together. It would be many years before we fully understood the depth of his philosophy and the often rocky climb to its integration. Basically, his Hierarchy of Needs outlines the ascending stages of development that he felt all people go through: the need for shelter, food, physical health, family, education, social integration and self-actualization. This last state – self-actualization – was defined as the highest state of spiritual awareness, the outgrowth of personal discipline exercised in a culture of love and compassion.

Our culture seduces us into a false understanding of love and marriage. This is reflected in the many unwholesome examples of marriage portrayed on television and in the tabloids. We see celebrated couples falling in and out of love with cyclical regularity and apparent ease. They enter into marriage relationships that last only until they meet the next leading male or female that sweeps them off their feet. Celebrities and royals too often influence our expectations relevant to the viability and longevity of the marriage dream. We want to see them realize the dream of married bliss. How often are we disappointed?

Our culture makes too little space for the heart in relationships. Just as your physical heart fulfills the function of reinvigorating your blood, so, symbolically, the energy of the heart can be engaged to bring new life to your relationship.

Without your conscious attention, your physical heart performs faithfully, loyally, and continuously. Likewise, the emotional energy of the heart is central to your continuous loyalty and faithfulness to each other. Keeping each other's hearts safe and protecting the precious balance of strength and vulnerability is the lifeblood of intimate relationships. Perhaps it's time to advocate for a new, heart-centered culture. How, we ask ourselves, can we introduce this warm, aspect of love into the public discourse and have it assume its rightful place? How can we give meaning to this reservoir of life that is so filled with emotion and feeling?

Committed relationship introduces major change – the rules for living are different. Expect your life to change when you begin to share the same home together. Likes and dislikes, annoying habits and petty irritations surface quickly and can dampen your bliss if you are not prepared. More relatives and new friends come into your life – all with their differing influences. With a little humor and lots of good will, you each learn to adapt to the needs of the other and quickly create your own couple style.

This is a time when you come to appreciate each other in new ways. Looking through your romance-clouded eyes, you each saw only the perfection of the other's mask. You saw only perfection because you each hid behind your own mask; neither wanted to see any flaws in the other. Perhaps you were afraid that your lover would discover that you were not all you appeared to be. Your expectations for each other were so high that naturally each must, in time, fall short of the other's expectations. When you come to see and accept each other as you are, your relationship begins to be more real.

We once attended a lecture given by His Holiness the Dalai Lama. Always one to laugh at himself, he wistfully recounted a story about a time in his early life when he was attempting to emulate a wise man. The wise man gave him very good advice; he reminded the Dalai Lama that when one tries to resemble someone else, one has to wear a series of masks to keep up appearances. The dutiful monk worked at being authentic, dropping the masks and finding his own style. When he tried to pass on this teaching to his followers, the results were quite revealing. Each heard what he needed so he could come out from behind the mask and transform his life for the better. The monk who always wanted to *take* began to understand *give*. The one who only knew how to *give* learned to *receive*. The doubting monk who wanted to *leave* got the message to *stay*. The reluctant one who never *spoke* was urged to go and *teach*. It was their willingness to be more real that caused their lives to make a complete turnaround.

There comes a time in our love relationships when we no longer need to keep up appearances. The changes can be intimidating. Our own experience with couples shows that they are able to keep the magic in their relationships by maintaining an environment of love and caring. Real caring includes a willingness to initiate and support change individually and collectively. When both agree to become students of marriage and begin to share their lives together the masks of pretense and unreal expectation drop away and their authentic selves begin to emerge.

Reflections

- Marriage is a fascinating journey of growth; there is much to learn.
- The path of true love is not always smooth; there will be obstacles to overcome.
- Skills for handling even the most difficult problems can be learned.
- As you begin to feel truly safe in the marriage, the masks come off.
- When expectation and pretense drop away, the authentic selves begin to emerge.

Take time to celebrate this new phase of your togetherness. You have both embarked on the greatest journey of your lives. You each travel your own path in your quest for awakening. It is your own soul-searching that ultimately frees you from the pain and confusion of life. Living in the moment, free from the fears of the past and without anxiety about the future, you are able to stay open to learning. The great gift of committed relationship is the willingness to assist with and participate in each other's growth. You can each be a mirror to the other. Learning to accept the mirror's images as true reflections of yourselves is a huge step in awakening as individuals and as a couple. The mirror honestly portrays what contributes to frustrations and doubts, just as it reflects what contributes to peace and clarity. It is easier to see what connects us to love and what separates us from it.

You have lovingly committed to partner each other on this path of love and awakening, but your growing bond of love may demand more courage, commitment and openness than you thought possible. Little by little you continue to discover the rich resources embedded in your deepest selves. The work towards self-actualization is a process of transformation, and when this path is unselfishly pursued, it empowers steady growth in both partners. With time, this commitment blossoms into the most exquisite of human relationships – a conscious, bliss-filled marriage.

CHAPTER 2

Waking Up to Unconcious Issues

You come to love not by finding the perfect person,
but by seeing an imperfect person perfectly.
SAM KEEN

The journey of waking up and living authentically presents its challenges. When we open our heart to our partner, feel deeply about him/her, we touch our own vulnerability. As we intimately explore what is magical and beautiful in the other, we sometimes touch the delicate unresolved pain that is at the core of our humanness. At the center of the human heart we discover the inevitable mixture of love and pain – theirs and ours. How many lovers have touched these most sensitive human emotions and felt confused? How often have they backed away thinking this can't be love? Others seize the chance to share their hearts in moments of deep connection, and to unveil their long buried pain as a ritual of opening to each other. It is in these tender moments of sharing our lives that we build intimacy and evolve our souls.

Love is the supreme nourishment of the heart. In the passion of love's intimate moments we feel completely alive. Our senses are heightened, emotions magnified; the excitement of life pulses through our veins. It is this ethereal experience of love's thrill that stirs our yearning to belong and to share ourselves with another. Nature's plan is exquisitely clever. It draws us together in a whirlwind of romantic passion where everything seems to be orchestrated for our happiness and pleasure. We think the whirlwind will last forever. It's nature's delightful little ruse to draw lovers together into the adventure of shared living, loving and learning.

The whirlwind eventually sets us down on terra firma. When the dust clouds evaporate, we begin to see things more clearly. The rose-tinted glasses come off and reality stands before us. It can be bewildering – even shocking – when we realize that the person we married does not quite conform to the flawless romantic image we had in mind. Some of the attractive traits we once admired in our lover now irritate us. The irritating imperfections we see in our partner are often reflections of those hidden aspects of our own personality that we have managed to keep closeted. It's just easier to see them in the other. That way we don't have to take responsibility for our flaws or make any changes. A little fear and anxiety creep in when we assume that our romanticized hero/heroine has feet of clay and may not be capable of offering us the comfort and care we long for.

This can be confusing for the heart-centered lover who doesn't want to expose his own vulnerability. It takes time to grasp the notion that his disillusionment doesn't spring from his spouse's imperfections or irritating traits, that the pain comes from his old emotional hurts. These unhealed wounds of the past become reactivated when his beloved unknowingly gets too close to his still hurting heart. In the unconscious marriage, this interplay results in covert struggles for power and dominance.

Transforming Our Past

> *Being deeply loved by someone gives you strength,*
> *while loving someone deeply gives you courage.*
>
> LAO TZU

Creating an intimate marriage involves reclaiming those aspects of ourselves that we have repressed, often from our childhood days. The gift of partnership is that we can effectively help each other heal from the unconscious issues that originated in our earlier life experiences. In fact, that is the very reason that we are drawn to each other. Our soul's natural instinct for wholeness and completeness beckons to our lover's soul and draws her into this magical and mysterious adventure we call intimate love.

Scars from our past are invisible to the human eye. Like psychological guests, they accompany us everywhere we go. Of course we can ignore them, pretend they are not there, or refuse to make their acquaintance. Dismissing the whole idea as psychological babble invites its own consequences for the host and his/her partner. How to free ourselves from these tyrannous hitchhikers is best illustrated in the following story.

Once upon a time, according to Irish folklore, a rich and tired old man called his two sons to his bedside shortly before he died. "Sons," he said, "I want you both to inherit the castle my father bequeathed to me. It is not in very good shape but surely together you can make it livable again." He handed them a huge leather binder stuffed with money. "I give this to you on one condition: you must live in the castle." The young men were delighted by their father's generosity. The eldest son finally asked his father why he had not told them about his inheritance and the reason why he had not lived in the castle all these years. The father replied, "You see, the castle has its own story, and everyone must experience it for himself. You are young and strong. Now go and make a home for yourselves there." Shortly thereafter, the old man passed away.

The two brothers had long conversations into the night. They were filled with mystery and intrigue. Shortly after dawn the brothers boarded their boat and set out for the castle. Just as their father had said, the castle was dilapidated; window sashes drifted loosely in the breeze, the walls were covered with a thick coating of green moss, the once beautiful shrubs now overgrown and gnarled. Inside, the floors were damp from the winter rains that managed to find cracks in the well-worn roof. They spent several hours exploring the old edifice. By nightfall, they felt exhausted and settled down to sleep by the light of an old candle.

Around midnight the elder brother awoke with a start – he heard weird noises, sounding like whispering voices. The noise got louder until it was almost deafening. Trembling, he jumped up and lit his candle. Words couldn't describe the pit of fear in his stomach when he saw the ugliest ghost hovering at the foot of his rickety old bed. Scared and frightened, he ran out screaming and took refuge in the gardener's shed. There he found his younger brother choking with fear and panic after enduring a similar experience.

Breakfast the next morning was sobering. The brothers pondered what to do with a haunted castle. Just then the old caretaker (who still kept an eye on the castle) rode up to the main entrance. The brothers shared their experience and asked the caretaker how they could possibly be freed of these unwelcome visitors. As only he could, he recounted the story of all the previous owners and their similar experiences with the ghosts. Not one of them could live there. The young men were incredulous but curious. "Is there anything we can do to chase the ghosts away?" they inquired. The caretaker explained that the only way to rid the castle of its old ghostly inhabitants was to face them and listen carefully to their whisperings. "Remember, don't fight them, don't run from them, just listen and follow their directions. They will leave."

Bold and brave, the two brothers settled in for the second night in their haunted castle. Sure enough, in the thick dark of the night, the ruckus started again. This time they were ready and each stood firm, though frightened. "Ghost, tell me your secret, so we can live here in peace." In surprisingly mellow voices, both ghosts repeated the same words. "Call me by my true name and I will never bother you again." A little less frightened, the young men continued to sleep in the castle while they renovated it over a period of several years. They inquired from relatives if any family members had died in the castle. No. The villagers, who knew the castle well, could not supply any names that pleased the nightly visitors. As hard as they tried, neither could come up with the true names of their ghostly lodgers.

The renovations complete, the brothers discussed the ongoing nightly saga and searched for answers. Finally, the younger brother realized just how much time and energy had gone into this investigation. He settled on the idea that these tormentors were just voices from the past that had taken on a life of their own because no one ever challenged them. The older brother agreed and was elated that they had finally solved the mystery. But how could they tell this to the ghosts? They were reluctant to confront them even though they wanted to be free of them. And then it happened. Each brother faced his unwelcome visitor and spoke the words that shed light on its identity: "You are the voice of my past." With that, the ghostly shapes gasped and disappeared, never to return.

We all live with the voices from our past. Some want to haunt us with stories about who we should be, what we should do, what we didn't get or what we don't deserve. If left unchallenged, these ghostly thoughts seem real and can run our life until we wake up and discover how illusory they are. Waking up is about becoming aware of our inner conversation – the inner dialogue that runs nonstop –

questioning its authenticity and having the courage to root out what is not true and real.

The first step in managing our emotional past is to make sure that we don't blame any one else, past or present. We did not have control over our childhood experiences, but we now have control over how we think about our past. Understanding how our mind and emotions work gives us more control over our lives.

When you came into your marriage you both brought all your unresolved emotional childhood issues (ghosts from the past) with you. When you fall in love, nature causes something fascinating to happen; an unconscious process of healing the unmet needs and hurts of childhood soon gets under way. Unconsciously, you have attracted this special person to help you grow towards wholeness. You didn't ask for this consciously, however a deeper part of you was searching for the right person to assist you in an amazing growth experience. Most couples are unaware of love's invisible agenda, because our culture does not honor the meeting of souls for this purpose within the context of marriage.

The seduction of romantic love has attracted you to the perfect partner to help you work out your unresolved issues in a safe, supportive environment. The early hurts originated in relationships can only be healed in a special kind of relationship. You have both found the perfect person who can help you transcend your unresolved childhood needs.

Remember, a bend in the road is not the end of
the road unless you fail to make the turn.

AUTHOR UNKNOWN

Incompatibility as a Building Block

Love is like a poultice that, when gently applied, can draw toxins to the surface. In time, one's partner will reveal those aspects of himself/herself that need to be resolved. When these anomalies inevitably show up, they are often misunderstood and can give rise to conflicts and problems. At this stage of togetherness, people often feel they have selected the wrong partner, and question how they could have made such a horrible mistake. Sure they had found the perfect person, they now doubt their choice. Mired in the abyss of conflict and struggle, about half of all married couples head for divorce at this crucial time. They do not realize – and no one has ever told them – that they have reached a vital and predictable point in the evolution of relationship growth.

Here, things can get tricky. Your issues are different from your partner's. Since we all suffer from some degree of emotional tunnel vision, we tend to think we have our own act together and if our mate would only do the same, everything in our world would be perfect. But the shock of discovering that your partner is not as perfect as you once believed sets the stage for the push/pull of ego domination and power struggles. Neither wants to let go of what was working so well during the hazy romantic phase of their togetherness.

Yes, he was the perfect person, but not in the way the unaware fledgling spouse understands. This unawareness leads to false conclusions. We generally attribute relationship difficulties to irreconcilable differences, and then go on to repeat the same mistakes with another partner. It is unfortunate that we are so unprepared and unaware of how relationships work. Such pain is avoidable.

Relationships begin to change when we understand that the partner we attract is a mirror image of those parts of ourselves that we would rather ignore or disown. Our unglamorous patterns cannot be stuffed away forever. One vivid example comes to mind. Susan, newly married, wanted to work on her fear of conflict. She avoided conflict like the plague, mostly retreating in silence at the slightest hint of disagreement. She finally became aware that as a child this was her only acceptable way of dealing with her father's angry outbursts. Realizing that in her new relationship of equals she had a voice to express her views and feelings, she was able to transform her past and handle disagreements with ease and without fear. As a result, the quality of communication with her husband was lifted to a whole new level.

Understanding how your past patterns can affect the quality of your relationship may help you to appreciate the interactions happening between you and your partner. When you are both aware of how this transformational process works, you can lovingly decide to assist each other in your growth. You can commit to sharing this experience in a spirit of empathy and acceptance. Then watch how true magic flows in your marriage. Real growth begins to transform your relationship. You are waking up and growing towards wholeness.

Transforming the past is a gradual process. You may not see results right away. But with understanding, love and mutual commitment, you can build real relationship. We have used a beautiful tool we discovered in the writings of Neale Donald Walsch; you might like to try it too. He says the nine words that can promote healing in relationship are: *I can understand how you could feel this way.* Next time you have a disagreement, reach deep within yourself and see if you can say these words with meaning. We have been pleasantly surprised at the results, and you may too. Notice, these words do not say *I agree with you,* or *you are right.* They simply extend understanding and that puts an end to the war of words, the collision of personalities, and opens the door to peace.

Finding Happiness

Are you among those who believe that it is your spouse's task to give you perfect love that answers all your needs and desires and keeps you blissfully happy? Do you believe that your partner's love alone will heal all your hurts and pains? The truth is that nobody can make you happy but you. In fact, nobody can make you happy or miserable but you.

You can experience true happiness when you maintain charge of your feelings; it's all about the choices you make from moment to moment. So when you run into difficult situations in your relationship, you have choices as to how you respond emotionally. When you experience times of serious unhappiness, your partner is not the problem. The difficult situation you are facing is not the problem. This person or that situation is never the problem. When you run into a circumstance that you perceive denies you happiness, you have simply come face to face with the reality that your perception of the event is the problem.

We all have our story about life: how it is, why it is, who and what made it this way. Our story is reinforced by our personal experiences, and we keep our story alive with our inner conversation. In fact, our whole life is lived in our inner dialogue. Since our life circumstances always reflect how we see, think and feel about life, there is no one else to blame for how it all turns out. The good news is that if we do not like the results, we can change our perception, make new choices and get different results. Check in with yourself, from time to time, to see if you are satisfied with your story; is it making your life better and helping you to solve your problems? If not, it's time to investigate your story.

Living is easy with eyes closed, misunderstanding all you see.

JOHN LENNON

Self-awareness

The capacity to be aware is a precious gift. It allows us to make choices by honing in on the possibilities open to us. It is only through awareness that we bolster the capacity to forgive and to grow through life's challenges. Awareness removes all distance and connects us to the heart of what is real. When you understand that your level of self-awareness stimulates your responses to events occurring in your relationship, you will see how important it is to be fully present to each other. You will see more clearly how your faulty perception of the event is the real cause of your unhappiness. Knowing this, you can take steps to change it. You can choose to respond in a more emotionally intelligent way.

Living and growing together gradually breaks open the protective armor around your heart and expands your capacity to love. You cannot give love until you first possess it. You cannot change the quality of your relationship without first changing what you know about yourself. It's what you know and feel about yourself and your own nature that will determine the happiness quotient of your life. The fastest learning curve happens in relationships. Your marriage will afford you ample opportunities to take a more honest look at yourself. An unaware self (personality or ego self) prompts one to pinpoint a partner as the cause of dissatisfaction. When this persists, marriages suffer and couples end up in constant struggle. The real solution can be found only within one's own awareness - seeing one's self as one truly is.

You have two natures: your real self and your unaware self. How you contribute and respond to situations in your relationship springs from your awareness of who you are and which self you are living from. The relationship dynamic is not the problem. When willing to yield to the vulnerability of love, your heart will reveal that your unawareness is the real obstacle.

No committed lover wants to hurt him or herself, or to suffer unnecessarily. You don't want to cause pain to yourself! Yet the fact is that individuals hurt themselves daily with eruptions of anger or fear. Others sink into dark holes of depression. In relationships, these emotional states take their toll on both partners. When you are unaware, you can hurt yourself and your partner on a regular basis. You may not mean to hurt your spouse; however, if hurt is happening, this is a good indication that you are still behaving unconsciously. When you come to understand this and catch yourself during your self-betrayals, only then can you mature emotionally and move to the next level of awakening.

Rita and Tony had been married for about three years. She worked as a nurse and was profoundly affected by the hurt and pain she dealt with every day. Tony was a computer salesman with a great love for golf. Given her irregular schedule and his frequent golf tournaments, they spent very little time together. He insisted that she attend his church with him and share his belief system. After complying with his wishes for three years (and feeling alienated from her own religious practice), she decided to be true to herself and stopped going to his church. Tony cajoled at first, then manipulated and ultimately threatened to end their relationship if she didn't change her mind. Rita took a vacation alone to help sort out her feelings. During her absence, Tony confided his dilemma. We asked him what was most important to him, persuading his wife in her religious convictions or saving his marriage. He confessed that it was purely his self-interest that wanted her at his church. But having a happy satisfying marriage was infinitely more important to him. We offered this advice; for one full month, do not mention church; cut back on your golfing activities; spend as much time as you can with your wife; ask her about what makes her heart sing and what dreams she has for the future; buy her flowers and take her dancing. Expect nothing in return. Let us know how things change for the better.

Rita did some deep thinking when she was away. She decided to put her heart and soul into her marriage and to stop finding fault with Tony. Their reunion was heartwarming and honest. Each promised to do better, every day the tension lessened and they had more time for each other. They talked more and shared their hopes and fears, and as their hearts opened to one another, they more easily saw their own shortcomings. The living environment became more pleasant and a joy to come home to. By holding only to what was real and true, they had a breakthrough. Priorities and attitudes were transformed, the power struggle ended and each found their peace. Many months later, we met

Tony again. "How are things at home, Tony?" we asked. "Couldn't be better," he replied, "and thanks for the advice. It worked. I realize now how my selfishness almost robbed us of the great life we have together."

Like Tony and Rita, we all need to be aware of our power struggles and find ways to end this unconscious way of living. If this is a pattern in your togetherness, be open to the idea that you may not know yourself as well as you thought you did. Most power struggles originate in the unconscious behaviors employed during the warm fuzzy glow of the romantic phase of relationship. As the masks drop off, we see our partner and ourselves in a new light, and this new honesty can cause us to fear that our needs will now not be met. So we manipulate, cajole, blame, shame, criticize and project on our spouse the very fears that lie buried in our own psyche. Looking through the murky lens of fear, the charming and attractive traits that drew us to our partner often become irritants. When we focus on his/her imperfections, the heart closes and we feel isolated and alone.

This feeling of separateness and aloneness contributes to the crisis of meaning in our postmodern era. It is becoming very apparent that narcissism (a much exaggerated preoccupation with self) is the most prevalent postmodern psychological disease. Too many of us are preoccupied with our own needs and wants. Our materialistic and self-serving relationship with life becomes a narcissistic indulgence in the demands of our personality. Our personality reflects what we feel and think, how we behave, what we value, in short, how we live our lives. The only way to end this self-centered relationship with life and love is to recognize and move beyond the separate sense of self (ego) that perpetuates it. It is this waking up to the truth of what is driving our life and relationships that frees us from the prison of our distorted personality into the aliveness of our soul. By way of analogy one could say: the sun is to the moon as the soul is to the personality. A culture driven by narcissistic tendencies is similar to the moon mistakenly thinking it is the sun. No warmth. No growth. No love...only chaos and confusion. This unconscious way of living undermines the building of sincere, honest, loving relationships. Moving into conscious living and loving is the work of transformation.

How do we find our way back to closeness with our real self and with our lover? The longing for connection opens the door to soul-searching, and affords us the opportunity to become aware of the aspects of our personality that we have not yet learned to love. Honest soul-searching helps us make sense of our past.

If you and your partner are locked in power struggles, each believing the other is at fault, and are unable to come to a fair balance of power, the answer lies in you. How often have you argued because you did not want your lover to think he/she was stronger than you? We live under the illusion that only the strong fight (they have something to defend?). Is it not more true to say that fighting only sheds light on the weakness of our ego and its inability to grasp the truth of a situation? The beauty of transcending our ego is that we see the wisdom of ceasing to project our shortcomings on our spouse. Instead, we take ownership of what is true about ourselves. Protecting our ego simply does not work, and changing partners is not the answer. You will continue to experience the same struggles until you uncover the cause, within yourself, and correct it. The affinity that called your souls together is a rich resource that will see you through these periods of growth as you learn to awaken to yourselves and each other.

Like all couples, we had to learn to balance our relationship. Our diaries from that time tell a story of reaching for this new phase of our togetherness by reminders of what we needed to do to grow together. *Become aware of yourself. Notice your reactions as you interact with those around you. Take charge of your thinking process. You are not your thoughts. You are more than your thoughts. You can learn to direct your thoughts and your emotions. This is the goal; this is what a truly self-actualized person does. It takes practice to live this way, but it is possible. Tune in to your real self. Become aware of your inner conversations. Uncritically observe your anxious states, your fearful states, and your negative states. These states are not your real self. They are your unaware or unconscious self in action.* These were some of the pointers we used to help ourselves remember the rules for waking up!

Let your marriage be a magical experience that refines
and transforms you both through your daily interaction,
and brings you both closer to all you are destined to be.

AUTHOR UNKNOWN

The path of awakening has unexpected twists and turns. Listening to our inner self as it glows in awareness and presents new possibilities is an art worthwhile cultivating. It helps to understand how our emotions can deliver a seesaw quality to our life and love. When we become aware of our thoughts (our inner world) we get a sense of why the world around us has taken the shape it now has. Each conscious or unconscious thought triggers an emotion. Our emotions are constantly changing according to our thinking; our emotions are our thought patterns experienced as our feelings. When we feel upset, it helps to understand that as soon as our thinking changes so will our feelings. Emotion is our body's internal reaction to the thought patterns in our mind. Our emotions can be nature's way of reminding us to keep watch over our thoughts. As often as possible, we need to remember to keep our thoughts aligned with the kind of emotions we desire to experience. We are in charge. So why not choose loving thoughts? Loving thoughts, combined with loving feelings, foster passion and aliveness in our life and relationships.

Experiencing the joys of awakened love is the reward for confronting your unconscious self. It is easy to recognize the unconscious self; it is always unhappy with something. You can be sure it will always manage to focus on the problems in your relationship, and life in general. It's the troublemaker. It's never satisfied, never content. When you awaken to this truth and mercilessly confront the negative self-talk, it will eventually recede out of your life. Ridding yourself of this negative inner chatter requires constant mindfulness.

Bridging Differences

The journey of the heart has recognizable signposts, markers and watersheds. The initial, romantic phase gives way to a more realistic view. Coming to terms with the new reality precipitates the struggle or balancing phase. This balancing phase can take time. So much depends on the willingness of both parties to balance their own inner sense of power, their ability to give and take in the interests of sharing and establishing equality, their openness to change, and their overall sense of self.

Sometimes a marriage gets stuck in this struggle mode; disgruntled partners bear the scars and recount the stories. "My partner just doesn't understand me," is the anthem of misguided couples that do not understand how to balance the energy of their togetherness. Numerous marriages never successfully navigate this slippery slope and end up in the emotional graveyard of despair and disillusion. Successful management of power sharing and a mature balance of roles and expectations have a stabilizing effect on relationships.

Faultfinding is the enemy of relationship. Avoid it – it's ugly! Never criticize your spouse. It helps to remind ourselves that we are not perfect either. See your partner as the beautiful person you love, as your perfect partner, not as a partner who is perfect. When you criticize you are likely feeling some inner discontent – and withholding spaces in your heart from your lover. It is easy to project your unhappiness as criticism. Finding fault with another usually means something in our inner world doesn't feel quite right. At those times it is a good practice to take a step back, look into your heart, and ask yourself why you are focusing on little things and missing the beauty and wonder of shared growth and togetherness.

Love will urge you towards a greater awareness
of yourselves as unique individuals.
WORDS FROM A MARRIAGE CEREMONY

Even though you and your spouse have committed to a growthful relationship together, you are still unique individuals, with strengths and weaknesses. Less than glamorous traits could be viewed as strengths in embryonic form. When you fell in love with each other, it was the total person you loved, the total impression or image you got of your lover. If you were to look at features in one person and compare them with features in another person, you would find that no two people are exactly alike. That is the mystery of creation.

When you see something in the person you love that is not precisely how you would like it to be, try not to focus on those flaws. Focus rather on the whole picture. Real love, mature love, accepts the whole person so unconditionally that the flaws recede. They're not necessarily flaws anyway – this labeling is a by-product of your perception. Finding the perfect partner just means attracting the right person with whom you share love as you grow and mature together. If your partner makes a mistake or is not as skilled or competent as you, it is wise to let your judgmental self take a back seat and practice being compassionate, gracious and gentle.

It takes awareness to realize that we are projecting our own shortcomings on our partner as we struggle to resolve old issues. This is the path that lovers take to become free from the past and open their hearts to love. Thus, our partner becomes a mirror to us of our own patterns. By recognizing and releasing these patterns, we can effectively end struggle and conflict. This work of transforming our past is one of the cherished rewards of shared love and soul growth. Differences are but opportunities to consider new ways of being in marriage, a wake up call to live more consciously.

Marriage is one long conversation, checkered with disputes.
ROBERT LOUIS STEVENSON

Conflict as Opportunity for Growth

Conflict is often viewed as the unwelcome intruder in relationships, although it need not be regarded as negative. Conflict, when handled wisely, can bring partners closer together. Did you know that couples in a great marriage have about the same amount of disagreements as couples that divorce? The secret is in how successful couples learn to manage their differences. Conflict and disagreements are part of the marriage journey and can't be avoided. In fact, if you create ways to avoid or suppress these challenges, it may be to the detriment of your relationship. Being in love doesn't mean you will agree on everything. Disagreements, when handled fairly, do not threaten marriage. On the contrary, it's important to learn how to disagree agreeably, or you won't be able to create an intimate relationship. Differences are part of every great marriage; the good news is that the skills needed to transform conflicts can be learned and used to enhance the relationship.

If you take the time to learn and practice the essential elements of successful relationship, and do it from a place of awareness, you will grow a strong bond between you and never have to walk away from your marriage. You will be counted among those who have successfully navigated the slope of intimacy and belonging by first balancing their own inner power, and together found ways to balance the energy of their relationship.

Reflective Questions

To help you deepen intimacy with your spouse, ask yourself the following questions:

1. Are you able to fully open your hearts to each other and share deep feelings?
2. How do you experience love when you are unhappy or lonely? Angry? Fearful?
3. Do you know how to stay connected during times of conflict and struggle?
4. Does your commitment waiver during difficult times?
5. Can you accept your partner without expecting that she/he change for you?

Waking up together occurs as we come to know ourselves and our partner at a deeper level. Only then can we balance the power in our relationship and grow closer. Our whole life can be a love affair provided we are ready to engage in the dance of life and allow it to absorb us. This requires our conscious commitment to the wonder and beauty of life and our willingness to embrace relationship with intention. William Doherty, speaking at the annual Smart Marriages Conference, described intentional marriage as one where *"the partners are conscious and deliberate about building and maintaining a sense of connection over the years."*

Rituals of Connection

Let's explore those rituals of intimacy and connection that help us sustain and enhance our partnership over time. These are ways to help us maintain and expand that sense of presence to each other, regardless of which phase of growth we are currently experiencing.

Every ritual between lovers is a way to celebrate love. We engage in connecting rituals every day even if we are not conscious of it. When we decide to use them consciously, they take on a new depth of meaning. A 'good morning' kiss or other love ritual (words or gestures) performed intentionally, has a sizzle that sends a clear message of "I love you". The good-bye kiss as you hurry off to your work life has a lingering effect. Even though your daily activity may keep you physically apart, you each know your heart belongs to the other and you are only separated by time and space. Why not interrupt your day occasionally to send greetings to your lover by phone or email? Never pass up the chance to re-enter your partner's world, to re-ignite the circuits that connect you.

Reconnecting after the workday is especially meaningful. This is a time for rest and relaxation, a time of togetherness. We kiss our lover hello to joyfully announce our homecoming. This, or some other welcoming gesture (you know best what you both enjoy), embraces you back into your shared living. How often have we been refreshed and renewed by the simple act of sharing the ups and downs of our day with the one heart that will listen compassionately and yet give balanced feedback where appropriate? This is the ritual of rebalancing our perspective and perhaps one of the most revitalizing gestures between committed partners. Close out the day with some ritual of affection – even a few minutes of close snuggling renews the message of love. If you are the one to initiate intimate rituals most often, keep doing it – your partner will love you for it and you will both reap the rewards.

Busy families with diverse schedules may not have the chance to ritualize the morning parting or evening reconnecting. They can, however, agree to set a time when they will connect; this can be the shared dinner ritual or a specific time in the evening when they can enjoy each other. Some daily connection is absolutely essential for the vitality and longevity of marriage. Statistics tell us that couples, on average, spend only ten minutes of personally meaningful time with each other daily. Sadly, without connecting rituals and shared time, we no longer feel the presence of our lover, our hearts shrink for lack of nurturing; we are in a relationship, yet lonely and alone. The promises of love and the beauty of shared living are sacrificed to the gods of duty, business, work, and a host of other seemingly essential endeavors. The price for neglect, carelessness, busyness, unawareness and thoughtlessness is diminishing intimacy and the heartache of love's dreams unfulfilled. If you have fallen into this trap, be the first to initiate new patterns of connecting. It's never too late to renew or restore heartfelt expressions of love even though they have to co-exist alongside work pressures and the stresses of daily living.

Why would a couple that lives and
sleeps together every night need dates and rituals?
Precisely because they live and sleep together.

BILL DOHERTY

Various types of rituals provide differing levels of satisfaction. Many couples derive great pleasure from weekly rituals of connection. The possibilities are enormous. Movie nights are popular, Sunday brunch or Sunday breakfast in bed and then read the newspaper or a good book together. Others take to the outdoors, cultivate a garden or enjoy sharing a hobby. We've heard couples share how they love to volunteer together, work out at the gym, attend classes or support worthwhile causes. The opportunities are endless – a little creative imagination will reveal what best suits your tastes and levels of energy. Whatever you choose, make it fun. Allow yourself to enjoy the benefits of both the anticipation and the satisfaction of your mutual interests. Time spent together deepens intimacy because it provides the chance to share yourselves with each other.

Vacation time is tremendously important for reconnecting and restoring waning passions. Whether you choose to simply relax with sun and surf or tour and explore other countries and cultures, be sure to bask in each other's warmth and communicate the sheer delight of your partner's company. Celebrate every event with genuine delight. This includes graduations, achievements in sports, music, the arts, etc. We all thrive on recognition and acknowledgment of our accomplishments. Ritualizing the other's success sends a message of pride and support.

We are all familiar with the ritual of celebrating birthdays. Make those days special for the one you love. Do something unexpected or unusual – something that will both surprise and delight your lover. Lovers of the world never forget to celebrate anniversaries – this can be in honor of the day you first dated, or your wedding, the day of your formal announcement to the world that you are committed in love. Plan ahead how you will ritualize this very important date. Honeymoon if you can, plan a romantic weekend away or celebrate with a very special romantic dinner. Of course, there are numerous possibilities that may delight you even more. If this requires special planning because of your schedules, start early. Never miss a chance to celebrate your love.

More Ways to Share Intimacy and Connection

Count your blessings. Often, in the rush of our daily living, we forget to notice the good and wonderful things around us. Regardless of how busy your lives become, take time out of each day to be grateful, to count your blessings for all the good things you have, the simple and the profound. Appreciate the wonderful partner you have attracted and show him/her your appreciation each day. Sit together from time to time and make lists of all the blessings in your lives. A grateful heart attracts even more good.

51

Have fun and laugh. Marriage can be serious work, but always remember to have fun and laugh. Laughter can provide comic relief when life becomes heavy and burdensome. Rent some funny movies. Watch the change they induce in both of you. Laughter rekindles enthusiasm and awakens the playful child in you. Pursue those recreational activities that evoke spontaneous fun. And do them often!

Bring value to yourselves. Read more books; meet interesting couples who are madly in love; attend seminars, retreats and workshops that focus on the joy of togetherness and the growth of mutual love.

Show courtesy. L. Mencken, when asked the secret to a happy marriage, replied simply, "Courtesy. That's the secret to happiness in marriage. I am convinced of it". A lifetime of successful marriage will essentially depend on that one word – courtesy. If you practice the ritual of being courteous to each other, you will maintain awareness of your marriage as something precious that can never be taken for granted. Courtesy will keep your marriage new and vital and your love fresh and fully alive. Take care not to fall into the unrewarding habit of taking each other for granted. Cherish the magic of respect and thoughtfulness.

The quality of our life, or relationship experience, is determined by the level of growth in self-awareness that we have attained. There is no limit to the levels of awareness or conscious evolution. In the premodern era, we considered that growth occurred when we healed our wounds or we resolved a problem. We were still dealing with the issues of the personality. (Most of us are familiar with the work of John Bradshaw, and others, and the healing of our dysfunctional past). The postmodern viewpoint is that as we confront the unresolved issues of our personality, our soul evolves itself and shifts to a higher level of consciousness. This is transformation. This is the process of waking up. This is the beginning of authentic living.

CHAPTER 3

Identifying Shared Values

⌒

Love is always bestowed as a gift –
freely, willingly, and without expectation.
LEO BUSCAGLIA

Marriage values are the agreed upon codes of conduct in relationship. They are the heart principles that permeate our relationship and our individual lives. Our values are our beliefs about how things should be, and our understanding as to how things are. We unconsciously acquire our values or beliefs from those who have influenced us. These include parents, educators, religious or spiritual teachers, and the society in which we were raised. Over the years, we select those principles that we believe are most important; they, then, become the guidelines for our behavior and decisions. We adopt them as the foundational codes or standards from which we live.

Common values are part of the reason that people feel attracted to each other. We don't necessarily talk about our values when we first meet – we're more likely to discuss common interests. It doesn't take long for values to become apparent. Let's take truth as an example. How truthful are you about your real past or are you likely to embroider it with little falsehoods about some grandiose accomplishments that rightly belong on your dream list? Sooner or later, the truth will become obvious – and then you may feel you have to lie to explain away this lapse of memory or unaccomplished feat! Benjamin Franklin once said, "I can see that the great part of the miseries of mankind are brought upon them by false estimates they have of the value of things."

To set the best foundation for a fulfilled marriage, it is important to define values to see how many of them are mutually shared. Some people go through life and relationships without ever assessing their basic values. A common set of values is necessary for peace and harmony in relationship. In fact, the repetition of actions and behaviors based on agreed upon values, forms the culture of a marriage.

Identifying Values

Having a mutually agreed upon code of conduct for your relationship can make living together more harmonious. If you both have well defined values and clear boundaries then you will better cope with the challenges or situations that arise. The attentiveness and presence of your partner in this discovery engenders trust and affords each the opportunity to decide jointly what has weight and worth.

We, the authors, stumbled into each other's value base in a

rather amusing way.

Austin's recollection: By the time I met Mary I'd almost given up on finding someone with whom I could share my life and who would love me for who I was. I had little confidence in myself as a lover, but I was very sure of my ability to be a strong and loyal partner. Loyalty was hugely important to me, as was fidelity. Although I was reserved around people, I had a good sense of humor. I paid little attention to money because I always had as much or more than I needed. My father taught us boys to respect women and to always do the right thing. The very first day I dated Mary, I shared my aspirations, very awkwardly, I recall, and was honest with her about my lack of experience. (Four years in a seminary offered no orientation in the ways of Eros or Romeo).

When I heard the story about Mary's background in a convent, I was reassured and felt we could learn to make music together. Quite frankly, I was captivated by her self-reliance; she exuded a confidence that was both sassy and inviting. She was quick, smart, petite and a stylish dresser. But most of all, I was fascinated by the depth of warmth and feeling that seemed to shine through her pretty face.

Mary's recollection: I met Austin at a decisive period in my life. My previous boyfriend of three months had left me just a few weeks before. I was no longer interested in men as reliable companions and the whole idea of relationship was indefinitely shelved. Austin and I had a couple of work-related meetings before we started dating. An interesting thought crossed my mind when he came to visit my office. He was tall, dark and handsome, a little reserved, but definitely polite and shyly charming. Could this charismatic man be the one who could wipe away all my misgivings about the male species? I quickly dismissed the idea.

Our first date was a turning point in my life. How easy it was to share my disappointments about men and to quantify what I sought in relationship. My priority was for a partner who was honest, trustworthy and open, as I believed I was. If I could find such a man, I was certain I would be committed, loving, giving and responsible. Sure I could be stubborn and opinionated, insecure and frugal, but I'd be willing to work at correcting these unattractive traits if I could just meet a decent, honest man with even a handful of the values I held dear.

It took several years for us to blend our divergent values around money, tardiness (respect for others' time) and relating to in-laws. We shared our differing experiences and perspectives, disappointments and expectations until we found common approaches that worked for both of us. When it came to love, we had very clear and similar values. We were fiercely loyal to each other. Austin was the more demonstrative one in the earlier years. It took Mary a little longer to feel reassured that this secure, loving life together had taken root and could be around for the long haul.

We learned the importance of taking time together to discuss our values and to identify the core ones. We encourage you to do this exercise for yourselves. See if you can agree on those values that you feel are most important to the success of your marriage. You might choose from the values listed below and add others that are important to you.

- Truth
- Love
- Honesty
- Respect
- Trust
- Openness

- Integrity
- Humor
- Commitment
- Loyalty
- Strength
- Courage

Select your values

At first glance, all the values may seem worthy to either one or both of you. Choosing your values in order of significance will help you to comprehend what is important to the other. Your combined values, honored and practiced, invite the energy of the heart to create the foundation on which to build a sustainable loving relationship. Think of any role models that you particularly admire and emulate. These can be people you currently know, or historical or mythological figures that inspire you to honesty, courage, strength or trust. Try to consider examples of how specific values would apply in your relationship.

If an example does not easily come to mind, then it's likely not a core value. When you have completed the selection process, list your agreed top five – in order of importance. Now discuss how you would express each of these top values in your partnership.

Shared values are pivotal to successful marriage. The more you practice sharing values, the more central they become to the life you are creating together. Daily reinforcement of these values strengthens your marriage. It helps build inner resources that can be called on when you confront the ups and downs of life together.

In time, it will become apparent how common values influence relational behavior. Harmonious relationships are built over time, fueled and nurtured by the strength of core values. Surveys show marriages that work best are ones where commitment and loyalty to agreed-upon values are espoused and practiced. Commitment to upholding the marriage contract and all of its values and beliefs is central to the growth and success of the relationship.

Love is no assignment for cowards.

OVID

Conflict can arise when your partner's values or beliefs collide with yours. You came into the marriage with a set of beliefs and so did your spouse. These may be radically different. Values are an accumulation of those beliefs collected over the years from parents, family, mentors, or friends. After checking out their validity in your life, you decided to give value to some of those beliefs and made them yours. They became the filter through which you see life. Now you are living with someone who had a different set of influences and beliefs that she has accepted as her view of life. So you each came with your beliefs – your book of rules for navigating through life.

Together you can create a common set of values, beliefs and expectations for your life as a couple. This is one of the first steps to take together towards building a strong foundation for a solid, long-term, happy relationship.

Reflections

- Can you accept that relationships are strengthened when you support each other's values?
- Do you accept that your core values are a major part of your identity?
- Consider how partners with widely different values may have more disagreements in their marriage.

Spiritual Values

The same heart that longs to belong also aches for spiritual exploration. Discussion of spiritual values helps both partners gain a deeper understanding of each other. Whether you belong to organized religion or follow a spiritual philosophy that nourishes your soul, agree on how you plan to take care of this vital aspect of your life. If you are fortunate enough to walk the same spiritual path, consider yourselves doubly blessed. Spiritual practice mutually shared adds a new level of intimacy to your togetherness.

Spirituality simply means living life with meaning, or perceiving deep meaning in the beauty of life itself. The linking of your souls is a spiritual and very intimate event. The heart, in its search for belonging, seeks out affinity and only pledges itself to the heart that echoes that same longing. This is one of the invisible mysteries of love. Trusting the mystery opens the door to belonging and satisfies our longing for intimate unity. This blending of souls in the shelter of each other's hearts is the real focus of the celebration we know as a wedding. We should indeed laugh and have fun and celebrate for a divine design is being shared with those who love and support the couple. When the public celebration ends, these two souls, now bonded in love and destiny, return to the private unfolding of the heart's secret wonders.

The Compatibility Factor

It may seem when you first fall in love that you have found a perfectly compatible partner. This, however, is very unlikely. Initially, you fell in love with a person on whom you projected your vision of the ideal partner. The romantic view of the ideal partner eventually gives way to a more realistic one. In the crucible of everyday experience we lower our expectations of each other and adapt to what is real. In the trenches of daily living we meet our true selves and become mirrors to one another. Mirrors reflect those blind spots in our soul that we ourselves cannot see. Within the invisible contract of marriage, we agree to serve as the eyes that see into the heart and fulfill the role of the messenger who faithfully reflects what needs to be discovered.

Moving beyond our current state of awareness requires honesty and willingness to change. Committed couples work towards this together as they continue to adapt to each other. Compatibility comes as a result of love and caring, the fruit of coming to know each other intimately. Happily married couples change and adapt together, creating their ideal relationship one step at a time. They know that discovering the mysteries of love is a joint endeavor.

The first duty of love is to listen.

PAUL TILLICH

Assessing and identifying shared values for evidence of compatibility will lead to new levels of awareness. You can check your compatibility levels by first taking stock of your differences. Are these differences significant? How do they affect your core values? Look at the areas where you differ from your partner. Have you begun the process of adapting to each other? How will you express your religious/spiritual values in the relationship? How will the expression of those values affect the partnership? Keep in mind that growth occurs for you and your relationship when you are willing to work through any differences. This soul-searching work serves to further deepen the bond of intimacy between you.

Valuing the Relationship with In-laws

Despite jokes about in-laws, nurturing a good relationship with your spouse's family can be very beneficial to your marriage. If you are willing to respect and show caring for your partner's family, this can go a long way towards increasing the joy of relationship. Remember the special person you love grew up in that family where those attractive qualities (the ones that impressed you) were cultivated.

Find ways to include your partner's family in the circle of your love. These could include acknowledging or admiring someone's qualities or talent. Take the time to learn about their interests; email or share information about their hobbies or pastimes. When you visit, bring a small gift or offer to help in some way. Show kindness and appreciation for their interest and hospitality. Family and home are the heart of our culture. Simple loving gestures are ways to invite her family into your home and your heart. Even if their values differ from yours, look for what you have in common and build on that.

Your partner will appreciate your efforts and respond in kind. When families open their hearts to each other, differences recede and holiday get togethers are easily arranged without the feuds and blues that so often mar holiday celebrations.

CHAPTER 4

A Vision for Your Marriage

~~~~~~~~~~~~~~~~

Dream lofty dreams, and as you dream so shall you become.
Your vision is the promise of what you shall one day be;
your ideal is the prophet of what you shall at last unveil.

JAMES ALLEN

Vision is the ability to plan the future with imagination and wisdom, creating a powerful mental picture of a desired future. In marriage, a shared vision is a statement of agreement between partners that determines what their ideal relationship will be. It provides focus for togetherness and inspires a joint commitment to achieve it.

Vision is the art of seeing things invisible.

JONATHAN SWIFT

Inspired visioning is perhaps the most sacred of all the art forms. By its nature, it creates active, living and moving forms that shift us temporarily into another world. This momentary glimpse into the invisible strikes a deep resonance within the sanctuary of the heart. Inspired visioning enraptures us and nourishes our souls. Excursions to the invisible (whether visioning or meditating) provide respite from the compelling harshness of the three dimensional world.

Visioning could also be described as practical dreaming. Take time for intimate sharing, and together formulate a vision of the quality of the marriage you desire to create. Visioning turns desire into design and then into full expression. It is necessary to have a focus for what you want to create together. With passionate direction you can achieve your dreams.

Most people think in pictures, and successful people use mental imagery to mentally design what they want to create in the world. We suggest that together, when your hearts and visioning are in alignment, you create a joint 'storyboard' or collage that will be a blueprint for the kind of marriage you both desire. It can serve as a 'preview of coming attractions' for your relationship.

If you can dream it, you can do it.

WALT DISNEY

Imagination is the power that allows us to form an image of our world. Using the research library of our mind we can create anything our heart desires. This is effective for creating all of the unique characteristics we would like to have in our relationship. It's a fun and engaging process for couples to do together. To effectively imagine your future is to feel that you have already achieved that which you want to be or have, and to identify yourself with that feeling until, in fact, it becomes reality. Remember, the outer world of experience is a direct expression of the inner world of thinking and feeling. When you align your thinking and feeling with having achieved what you desire, you will, according to the degree of your desire, draw to you the desired reality.

Imagination is more important than knowledge.

ALBERT EINSTEIN

Ancient philosophy has long held that mental imaging is the doorway to reality; with this power we have the ability to create the life we desire. By engaging the inner world of imagination we formulate our desire. Holding and affirming this inner vision, we attract the conditions that cause our desire to be made manifest in the outer world. It is important to become fully aware of the role this power of imagination has in our life. It is crucial to understand the relationship between the inner activity of the mind and feelings, and the reality of our life and relationship. The inner world is the world of cause while the outer world of experience is the effect. Our outer world, with all its experiences, is but a visible out-picturing of our inner mind's state. To change the outer, we must first change the inner. With appreciation and right use of imagination, we can accelerate the journey to a mature, loving relationship.

Athletes are a striking example of the power of visioning. Tiger Woods sees himself as a highly successful world-class golfer. Before he plays, he imagines the entire course in his mind and how he will execute at each hole. He said in a television interview, "At the end of every tournament I review every stroke and hole to see what I can learn from the experience." That then becomes the image of success for his next round.

Likewise, if you imagine yourselves living in a magnificent dream home, and stay in that awareness and really believe it to be true, that awareness over time will lead you to the object of your strongly held vision. This happens when you mentally accept what you desire. When you think from the state of already having achieved what you want, you achieve success. The secret is to start with the end in mind; think from whatever you want. Visioning is the process of applying imagination in an organized fashion. The opposite of mentally creating your future is passively accepting life as it comes to you, which often results in disappointment. Remember, achieving what you want for your marriage is an art and a science; your ideal marriage will not happen by chance.

Once you have agreed on and selected a vision for your journey together, write it out in detail and put it in a place or places where you can read it daily. Repetition increases the likelihood of success.

When you have visioned how you would like to experience your relationship, build a mental image of a scene that would evidence the fulfillment of your dream. Reinforce your image with feeling, and experience it as a present reality. Do this as though you have, in fact, achieved the ideal marriage , and experience in your minds all that comes with it.

Create an Image Board

*Love does not consist in gazing at each other
but in looking together in the same direction.*

ANTOINE DE SAINT-EXUPERY

Because you are creating your life and your relationship with the images you hold in mind, it's helpful to create a collage or image pages. An image page is made by cutting out words and pictures (use magazines, travel brochures, photographs) that represent your ideal life together. Paste these words and pictures on pages or on a poster board and arrange them to illustrate how you would like your lives to be. Create images that reflect the look and feel of what you desire.

You can create images of various aspects of your relationship that you would like to see enhanced. Create images that describe inner qualities you want to develop such as self-confidence, personal awareness or spiritual growth. These images or words can be organized to fit around pictures of your ideal home, furnishings, cars, vacations, etc.

Remember to keep your visualizing positive and always in the present tense. Use images and affirmations that help you experience the feelings of success in the *now*.

Assembling Your Image Board

The image board will unfold from your creative selves and will help you stay focused on your true goals. In this activity, it helps to put the rational mind aside just as you do when you sleep and dream. Constructing an image board is the process of creating your dream life. Begin by putting a photo of you both together in the center of your image board so that what you are imaging is truly for yourselves. Place all your symbols, cutouts, pictures, and words in groups on the poster board seeing how they work together. Arrange them so they fit well visually. Just start playing with possibilities as you group images together. Check to make sure that your visioning reflects all your goals as already achieved.

When Cindy and Don created their image board they wanted a picture of a sports car they imaged having in the future. They specifically wanted a red car but the car dealer's catalogue showed that model in silver only. So the picture of the silver colored car was glued in place on their image board. A couple of years later they visited the dealer's show room. The car was no longer produced in red, but they were offering a fantastic deal on a silver one. The couple could not believe their good fortune and happily settled for the sports car of their dreams – in silver as their image board had shown!

Understand that you are describing yourselves and your relationship the way you hold them in your heart and want them to express. The fact is that all the qualities needed to create this already exist in both of you; visualizing simply emphasizes those aspects of yourselves that have the ability to turn desires into reality. Every time you look at your image board, don't only see it and read it, internalize it by feeling it to be true. Get excited about it and live from the truth that it has already been created. When your heart generates real passion about it, your beliefs and feelings will help to accomplish your dreams with ease.

Exercise

When you have completed your image board, take some time to journal your feelings imagining that you are already living the life you have pictured. In your mind's eye your dream marriage has now been realized.

- Describe what this means to both of you.
- How has your life been changed?
- What did you have to overcome?
- What was your greatest learning?
- What made you persist?
- What does love mean to you now?
- Journal the transformation that has taken place in you since you created your image board together.
- Write a letter to your spouse expressing how you now feel about your marriage.

If your marriage is not living up to your dreams, if you feel like you have grown apart, that you lack satisfaction, it's never too late to re-vision your dreams. Looking through the eyes of love, you remember that this is your life to orchestrate as you both wish. You have power over the kind of relationship you create. This is your opportunity to tune into each other, and make new choices. What kind of life do you want to enjoy? What magic do you want to create together? What wonder do you want to experience? When you know what you want, and are willing to put your heart into it, you can experience love and romance, caring and companionship and a deep sense of fulfillment.

CHAPTER 5
Journey of Discovery

⌒

Love cannot endure indifference. It needs to be wanted.
Like a lamp, it needs to be fed out of the oil of another's heart,
or its flame burns low.

HENRY WARD BEECHER

The human body longs for the presence and nurturance of its mate. When you first discovered each other, the affinity of your hearts and souls issued a silent invitation to enter each other's presence. The language of the human body longs for the intimacy of human touch. The dimension of your lives changes as you attract each other into a journey of discovery.

One of the markers along the path of conscious loving is the awareness that many of the difficulties that arise in marriage are signals that some need of one or both partners is not being nurtured. Some of us have never fully experienced the presence of compassion. We have not allowed ourselves to be touched by the outstretched heart of another in a gesture of encouragement. Unwittingly, we have denied ourselves this most precious sharing. We remain locked in the prison of our own confusion, shriveled and parched for the presence and warmth of heartfelt compassion. An intimate relationship is the safest sanctuary for touching compassion and thus finding the exit door from a closed heart.

A conscious marriage thrives in the rich soil of a giving environment where each partner wants to be fully present to the relationship. The key question becomes, "What can I give to my partner as my contribution to creating a loving, intimate relationship?" As you give, so shall you receive. Your relationship will thrive when each partner feels acknowledged and nurtured. It is wise for your partner to be fully aware of what makes you feel that you are loved, acknowledged and cared for.

Marriage is our last, best chance to grow up.
JOSEPH BARTH

Celtic folklore thrills with delightful tales about life and love. One of our favorites is the story about the King and the Beggar. As the story goes, there once was a king who went to war to protect his kingdom. Knowing the danger of war, his beautiful wife stayed home. But her husband, whom she adored, was gone for a very long time and she pined for his return. Broken hearted, she fell ill and no medicine could save her. When this news reached the king's ears, he immediately returned home. Alas, his beloved wife had slipped away. His days were long and lonely and no one could console him. Princesses came from other kingdoms to visit, but he refused to see them. His advisors were sure the king would find happiness again if only he would consent to meet with these prospective companions.

One sultry, summer evening when the king was dining in his

palace, a shabbily dressed old man knocked at the gate and asked to see the king. The servants refused, but the man insisted that he be allowed to offer a gift to the king. Upon meeting the monarch, he gifted him with a basket of fruit. The king graciously accepted the poor man's gift although he had no need of it for his orchards were filled with a variety of ripe fruits. His butler was instructed to toss away the fruit but keep the basket. Nevertheless, the old man went away content. A few weeks later, the same thing happened and the fruit was tossed away again. On the third visit, just as the old man handed the basket to the king, a nearby archer missed his target and the stray arrow knocked the basket to the ground. The contents spilled all over the courtyard in front of the king. Inside the basket was filled with precious pearls. The two previous gift baskets were quickly checked and, lo and behold, they too were lined with pearls. The king was astonished at the beggar's generosity and offered to give the man anything his heart desired. With that the beggar ripped off his tatty clothing and there stood a beautiful woman. "I ask nothing less than to live in your kingdom and to bring back the joy you lost when your beloved wife died of a broken heart," she said. "Very well," replied the king, "because of your generosity, you shall be my royal guest." Almost immediately, a new joy was felt throughout the palace. The king regained his interest in music and hunting. He lavished his new guest with magnificent gifts. Not many months later, wedding bells rang throughout the kingdom and the couple lived happily ever after.

This story conveys vividly that even the greatest challenges can bring gifts of new growth. Sometimes we push away or refuse to meet the circumstances or opportunities that can open us up to a greater experience of life. Often, our greatest pearls of wisdom and happiness come disguised as ordinary, unwanted, or unnecessary. When we are willing to stay open and to embrace whatever life brings, nurture it with care and look for its hidden meaning, we thrive. This way, our real needs are always met.

Discovering our Needs

All of us, from time to time, have problems understanding the ebb and flow of our own emotions. It is no wonder that the issue of emotional needs is such a major factor in marriage. Our longing for the liberating intimacy of human touch can be satisfied in a number of ways: some love affectionate gestures, others enjoy admiration and support, while others feel closest in the rapture of sexual intimacy. Don't be surprised if your preference is for deep meaningful conversation, the sharing of your deepest self. Honesty and openness, companionship and a spiritual outlook on life may top the needs of others. For some, the willingness to share responsibility for both domestic and financial matters brings them closer together. None of this would feel complete without a sense of commitment from our partner. We only want to entrust our heart and our dreams to that special someone who is committed to be present and with whom we can build a life together.

When these needs are not identified, shared and met, it often results in hurt feelings, a vague sense that something is missing and a propensity to hold the other responsible. Most couples are somewhat unaware of each other's needs. Cultivating a sense of presence, opening your hearts to each other, is a sure way to become conscious of your partner's needs. Conversely, unawareness of unmet needs is the primary culprit for ongoing struggle in a large number of relationships.

The attraction and seduction of feeling close can engulf us and cause us to lose ourselves if we are not emotionally healthy. The reason is very simple; as much as we need and enjoy closeness, we cannot ignore our other basic need for personal space. A happy balance of closeness and individual identity is the hallmark of successful partnering.

We dance alone,
We dance together,
We move each other
Into rhythm.
AUTHOR UNKNOWN

When partners feel loved in the ways that most fulfills them, there continues to be a giving and receiving that allows them to experience deeper feelings of acceptance and intimacy.

Men and women have differing emotional needs. Giving to your partner what you like to receive doesn't necessarily satisfy him. You may have the best intention in your giving, but your gifts may not be as appreciated as you'd expect. It is important to discuss your needs and desires honestly to avoid disappointment and hurt feelings. Satisfying those needs goes a long way to nurturing a contented spouse who feels truly loved.

The nurturance of emotional needs by either partner enhances the relationship, and with each loving gesture, love and caring are deepened. On the emotional level, each caring gesture increases the love quotient of your marriage. Conversely, when you fail to satisfy the other's need, your love quotient suffers a withdrawal. Take time to discover your own and your partner's emotional needs. As a starting point, consider the following and check how well you give and receive love to your partner in these ways.

- **Acceptance** – frequent compliments, positive encouragement, respect and courtesy that empowers and inspires and shows a genuine acceptance of your spouse.
- **Affection** – emotionally connecting, intentionally nurturing your partner with romantic caring, kindness, kissing, etc.
- **Attractiveness** – taking care of appearance, dressing attractively, paying attention to weight, etc.
- **Conversation** – meaningful self-sharing that includes listening to each other to really understand what is being said.

This way you come to know each other deeply, and stay interested in all aspects of your partner's life.

- **Commitment** – to being 100% present to each other, to fidelity, to individual growth, and to nurturing a great marriage.

- **Companionship** – sharing interests, activities, hobbies and lots of fun times together. Interests shared in a fun way build togetherness and closeness.

- **Honesty and openness** – never keeping secrets from each other. Trust is built when spouses share thoughts, feelings, likes, dislikes, concerns, fears, etc.

- **Sexual satisfaction** – enjoying uninhibited sexual passion, learning and exploring how to pleasure each other. Intimate touch deepens the sense of belonging.

- **Sharing household responsibilities** – cooking, cleaning, decorating, etc. In most successful marriages, couples share the household responsibilities. It's another way to actively show love towards each other.

- **Sharing financial responsibilities** – spending, paying bills, handling savings, investments, etc. This is a sure way to build financial security and avoid one of the biggest traps for conflict in marriage.

- **Spiritual sharing** – celebrating the sacredness of your marriage. Ideally, you are both on a similar spiritual path, or at least supporting your partner's spiritual journey.

There is nothing more admirable than two people who see eye-to-eye
keeping house as man and wife, confounding their enemies,
and delighting their friends.

HOMER

In a conscious relationship, partners joyfully seize every opportunity to empower and to encourage the full expression of each other. In an unconscious relationship, immature egos become emotional destroyers and disempower the partner. Emotional sabotage replete with destructive behaviors, if left unchecked, will erode and, in time, destroy a relationship. Be aware of employing any destructive behaviors. Partners who employ disempowering tactics are unconsciously trying to change their partner through external control and manipulation. These behaviors impact the sacredness of the marriage contract, sometimes irrevocably.

Destructive behaviors to avoid: criticism, blaming, complaining, threatening, anger and jealousy.

Criticism

The compassionate heart affords no shelter to criticism. No one enjoys criticism even when they admit that they have done something wrong or foolish. If you feel irritated or angry because of your partner's mistake, resist the urge to lash out. Check first within yourself to see what is irritating you. This kind of self-discipline will cause your partner to feel grateful and increase his/her level of respect for your empathy. This is a sure way to build up the love quotient in your marriage. On the other hand, you create a massive love withdrawal if you lash out in demeaning criticism, wound another's sense of self, stir up old resentments or erupt in rage. By taking ownership of your annoyance, you avoid the need for defensiveness and the face-saving reactions of denial or self-pity. A mature response to criticism is to treat it as useful input and an opportunity to grow personally. This generosity of spirit is acknowledgment of the truth that there is something new to learn. It has a further benefit; this may be the piece of information that finally frees you from fear and self-deception. (You did not see yourself that way, and never thought anyone else might either). Imagine how your relationship would blossom if you could harness the courage to say, "I can understand how you could feel that way." The war of words ends; the clash of personalities ceases, and peace begins.

Blaming

Blaming is a form of self-defense and an unwillingness to take responsibility for one's actions. It's an unconscious way of projecting one's unresolved issues onto the other. Blaming escalates conflict and prolongs the notion that in order to be right the other must be wrong. This is faulty reasoning at best and a good breeding ground for resentment. If you consistently put being right before being happy, soon you'll be learning to be happy by yourself. The way out of blame is simply to acknowledge the issue at hand and make friends with the two magic words, "I'm sorry."

The unwritten rule in the unconscious relationship is to face as little as we can and avoid as much as we can. Every time we face an issue rather than avoid it, we grow in stature. The lessons of life show up consistently and we keep bumping into that reality until we get the message. Life will continue to give us everything we need and nothing can stand in its way.

So, the next time your spouse comes bearing good news about some hidden greatness in you that you could not see, graciously take ownership of it and be sure to find a way to connect with your lover's heart.

Complaining

Complaining evokes a tightness of the heart. It includes fault finding, nagging and sometimes insulting your partner. It's focusing on the small part that is not working and overlooking the larger parts that are working well. If there is a genuine problem, get specific about it and work together to find a mutually acceptable solution. Make an agreement that whenever you present a complaint you will offer at least one possible solution. This puts complaints at the level of challenges to be solved rather than opening the door to relive everything you are dissatisfied with. The ability to solve problems together builds reliance in the partnership.

Let's suppose your spouse complains that you watch too much television and don't attend to the household chores. Deep down you know this is true but you make excuses and deny the honesty of the complaint, which further annoys your partner and the war of words goes on. No peace and no growth.

How much do you think your relationship would improve if you tried something new? Would your spouse be happier and would you both be more peaceful if you replied, "Honey, you know I've become aware of that lately. Let's talk about how we can take care of these chores so we can both be happy."

Threatening

Threatening is an attempt to wound the heart. No matter how difficult things become, never, ever, threaten the relationship. Avoid language that implies you are leaving, that the marriage is not worthwhile, and divorce is the only answer. The most destructive aspect about threatening is that it jeopardizes the security and safety of the marriage. Trust is eroded. Additionally, threatening has the potential for explosive conflict, verbal and psychological abuse. The damage ravaged on the marriage in a few short seconds of uncontrolled behavior may take weeks, months or years to repair. This is one of those times when your aware self must come to the rescue. Until it does, retreat may be the fastest and least destructive option. Retire to a quiet, private place in your home and collect yourself emotionally. Use one of the Stress Relieving techniques (see Chapter 7) as a way to discharge the tension and regain peace of mind. Ask yourself what it is that you fear losing so much that you need to threaten your lover so you can have it. It helps to remind yourself how much you love your partner and how emotionally committed you are to seeing love in every situation.

Later, you can approach your partner in as loving a way as you can muster, and attempt a new dialogue (after you have made profuse apologies) by asking, "What is the real hurt?" Use the Couples Dialogue (see Chapter 6) to unravel the situation. This can be done without one losing face, blaming, or shaming the other. The offender will appreciate this maturity and generosity of spirit. Apologies for the offending behavior are definitely in order before any new dialogue can be initiated. Agreements need to be made on how to handle future frustrations without threatening; this works best when both agree that this expression of behavior is unacceptable.

Anger

Anger is an emotion that is often misunderstood and mislabeled. We are all familiar with the fierce presence of anger in ourselves, or in others. We resent it and try to avoid it without fully understanding its nature. Psychologists tell us that anger is often a camouflage for other emotions that we unconsciously feel might expose our vulnerability. We are scared to touch or expose our feelings of fear, sadness, loneliness, inadequacy, protracted irritation, etc. Repeated denial of such feelings stuffs them down into a reservoir that in time becomes negative, painful and overloaded. Eventually the reservoir, unable to contain its cargo, explodes in an angry outburst. This is triggered by as little as a misguided remark or as much as some untenable burden too heavy to bear.

Resorting to anger as a response to life's challenges is a sure sign that we are not being real with ourselves; we are disconnected from the energy of love. The expression of anger could be a call to reconnect with our true self, and the depth of feeling that we have successfully ignored or numbed. Trust your heart to help you sort out your feelings; you can be guaranteed of non-judgment and compassion. Then be willing to investigate the truth of why you react the way you do. Do this for yourself and your partner. Be aware of yourself when you express your anger through the 'silent treatment' or through complaining and nagging. You will feel more powerful if you can regain control and discuss things calmly. However, if you need time to cool down, at least have an agreement between you about the rules of mutual respect.

Never attack the other person in a destructive manner. Wait until you are able to acknowledge the truth about your thoughts and feelings, and share these without losing control. If you must express your feeling of hurt, disappointment or rejection, (or any other feeling) resolve to do it in a non-threatening way. Abuse of any kind is unacceptable because it disrespects the very essence of your partner. We have observed that the majority of couples who adopt an attitude of zero tolerance for any and all categories of abuse eventually work out their problems satisfactorily.

Bruce and Sandra had been dating for almost two years before the question of marriage came up. Bruce hungered for stability and felt Sandra might enjoy that too. Yes, she loved her man, but the thoughts of a long-term commitment to him made her nervous. Bruce's angry episodes left her fearful and distant. She expressed to him how flattered she felt that he would want to spend his life with her, but explained that she could not marry him until he dealt with his anger. Anxious to move forward with the relationship and to find peace of mind for himself, he sought help.

After some deep soul searching Bruce realized that for most of his life he had been angry. Something always provoked his anger. People remarked on his fiery temper and quickly scattered when it flared. He was bitter about the unfair hand life had dealt him. For a long time, he was silent about his father abandoning the family, leaving his mother to cope and survive. A fatal automobile accident ended his mother's life just as she had found a new love. It was then that his brooding silence turned to anger. He couldn't accept the injustice of it all. If he couldn't find justice then he wanted revenge. Life became increasingly difficult for Bruce as he used his discontent to manipulate those around him. He felt most alive when he was raging. Somehow life would have to come to him on his terms. Friends and family gradually distanced themselves.

Slowly, Bruce began to understand Sandra's reluctance to his proposal. It became clear to him that nothing oppressed him more than the memories of what happened. He decided he had learned enough from his anger and it would no longer control him to the point where he could make no other choices for his life. He committed to himself to take back his integrity and to stop giving away his power to people and systems who were least deserving of it. This conviction to free himself from the past opened the door to a new way of living. In short, his understanding of his anger and his willingness to work through it was the breakthrough that changed his life.

Bruce shared this soul searching during our mentoring sessions. He felt that confronting his past and breaking free of it was the most rewarding thing he had ever undertaken. Sandra was equally elated that she had the courage to point out the shortcoming in her lover and stand by him as he worked through it. They came to explore how to grow together as a couple. A very contented Bruce and his supportive fiancé planned a wedding for later that year.

Working through Power Struggles

Despite our best intentions, power struggles, misunderstandings and misplaced remarks can find their way into our interactions. This gives rise to the war of words. Practice checking in with yourself to discover which vulnerable facet of your personality has been offended, and why. The key to de-escalating conflict is to think about and talk about how to handle disagreements before they occur. If you discuss how you'll resolve them then it's unlikely you'll get out of control. This works best when both parties agree to practice mutual respect.

Agree to express feelings on an on-going basis and so avoid the need for angry outbursts. Clarify what you're perturbed about. Ask yourself if you are overreacting to a fear that something is being denied you or that something you have might be taken away. If you are overacting, call a time out and agree to a specific time and place for resuming your discussion, (never the bedroom). Re-open your dialogue with words such as, "I need to share my feelings with you about…" Objectively explain the behaviors that offend you. Be clear as to the behavioral change you would like to see. Indicate why you would appreciate the change and how it could improve your relationship.

Make "I" statements as you share your feelings openly and honestly. Be aware of your partner's feelings. The listening partner must be sure not to ridicule or discount the angry partner's feelings. Settle on a new understanding and make agreements for going forward. Show appreciation for the new understanding. Move into forgiveness for your partner. Check in with yourself to understand the deeper emotion behind your anger. Never pass up the chance to confront your issues and liberate yourself from their grip. Probe to find out what it is you fear losing and how your life would be without it.

In this place of honesty the reality of the situation will surely surface, and you will free yourself from this burden. If anger and arguing are excessive, agree to get professional help.

Jealousy

Jealousy is a state of fear that arises from suspicion or envy caused by a real or imagined threat to what one holds valuable. These feelings arise when we fear that our lover has betrayed the safekeeping of our heart. Jealous feelings may be provoked by rivalry, as in the case of a lover's flirting with others. Jealousy can be extremely painful and rob the relationship of its joy and safety. It skews our perspective to the point that nothing in the marriage seems right. Hurt feelings often drive us to shut down our hearts and withhold our love. The pain of possible betrayal diminishes our trust in our partner. A good antidote is to be open and honest and ask questions that will clear up the real or imagined withdrawal. A gentle approach works best especially when the grounds for suspicion often prove to be unfounded. If you proceed with love and a genuine care for protecting the marriage, you have a better chance of resolving this situation peacefully and with minimal damage.

Exercise

When you feel awkward about verbalizing your needs, write a

love note! The following example will serve to generate ideas.

My Dear   _____

Thank you for all the love you share with me.

(List the many ways you feel loved and cared for)

I feel really loved and cared for when you:

_____

_____

_____

_____

_____

I would feel even more loved and cared for if you would:

_____

_____

_____

_____

_____

_____

It feels so wonderful that we can create such an honest environment for sharing our love.

Please let me know how I might show you more of my love and care for you.

Your Lover _____

Lovers' Insights

How well do you know your partner's likes and dislikes? A time of discovery together can be enlightening - and fun too.

What is your partner's favorite or most important?

- Book
- Pleasure
- Hobby
- Flower
- Food
- Place to visit
- Color
- Way to relax
- Way to experience love
- Dream for the future
- Life Goal
- Type of Work
- Way to have fun
- Place to shop
- T.V. show
- Thing to learn

Take the time to discover more of your lover's needs. This information equips you to better accommodate those desires. It also assures that your gifts or surprises will be fitting and warmly appreciated.

Sharing Appreciation

In surveys, men and women both reported the need for appreciation. This may be expressed in a variety of ways – loving gestures of kissing, hugging, compliments, gratitude, gifts, flowers, etc. The possibilities are only limited by your level of creativity. In growthful marriages, couples find ways every day to show appreciation for each other. Share with your partner the ways you would like to be appreciated. Become aware of the positive ways you encourage each other – and do it often. Acknowledge each other's strengths. Compliment your partner's growth and offer encouragement to evolve in those areas that are still underdeveloped. Appreciation attracts appreciation; always look for the positive in each other. Say "thank you" for thoughtful gestures. Take nothing for granted. Develop a sense of humor – it's a powerful state changer. Do those little things that you know give pleasure to your lover. Spring a loving surprise and enjoy the results! This is how you enhance the quality of your relationship.

One couple, in response to being asked how they keep their marriage exciting and new, responded, *"We continue to romance each other - treat each other like the lovers we were when we first courted. All family responsibilities aside, we focus on each other and enjoy the attention. We both love to give to each other because in love you can never out-give your partner. When we feel loved we respond with love. In today's hectic lifestyle we have to steal moments for sharing. It isn't always easy, but we steal them anyway. It's been our agreement from the beginning that we each take 100% responsibility for keeping our relationship alive and interesting. We discovered that when we take the focus off our own needs and attend to each other's, we quickly find our needs are well taken care of."*

CHAPTER 6

The Language of the Heart

⌒〜⌒

Communication is to relationships what breathing is to life.

VIRGINIA SATIR

Communication – the mutual exchange of both thoughts and feelings – plays a significant role in healthy relationships. The free flow of ideas clearly expressed within the couple's shared lives shapes the vitality of their togetherness. Clear, open communication promotes growth, healing, closeness, and provides a reservoir of understanding that can be tapped for problem solving and conflict resolution.

Communication includes speaking and listening. Listening is an act of presence often overlooked and hugely underrated. When we listen attentively to our partner, we take in his/her voice with all its inflection and subtle meaning. In marriage surveys, communication problems usually show up at the top of the list. Although the importance of effective communication skills is clearly acknowledged, (68 % of all couples seeking help cite this as their biggest issue), most of us never learn how to communicate consistently well. And yet, the quality of our relationship is largely determined by the quality and skill of our interactions – both verbal and non-verbal.

Communication Takes Place on Many Levels

Imagine this scenario: A husband comes home a little late and his wife says, "Why are you so late getting home? You didn't even call to let me know." He not only hears the words but also experiences other messages in the tone of her voice, body posture, and facial expression. If she has ever said these same words to him, the meaning of those remarks in the past will color how the message is received in the moment. He wonders just what response she might be looking for when she makes that statement. Is she meaning that she missed him, does she want an apology for his being late, or does she simply want affection? What he experienced during the time he was away from her will also affect how he interprets the message. Even simple exchanges can get complicated. Both partners are sending and receiving verbal and non-verbal messages at the same time. Successful relationships are built when we practice clear communication in affirming and effective ways.

When marrying, ask yourself this question:
Do you believe that you will be able to converse well with this person
into your old age? Everything else in marriage is transitory.
FRIEDRICH NIETZSCHE

The Art of Listening

Listening is the invisible meeting place in successful communication. Yet, we so often feel our partners don't listen to us. Many couples live in virtual isolation from each other, their hearts estranged and the depth of their longing denied. In previous generations living room furniture was organized so that people could sit facing each other and enjoy conversing together. Have you noticed that in most homes today living rooms are set up so that everyone sees the television? With television as the focus, we are distracted from each other. And although we still speak, our hearts are often absent and few of us actually communicate effectively.

Communication is an art that needs to be learned and practiced. Perhaps we like to discuss things and exchange facts and opinions. However, there is a difference between discussion and conversation. A discussion is essentially a cerebral exchange of ideas. A conversation is an exploration of another person's thoughts, experiences and feelings. Conversation builds friendships. Conversations are an essential ingredient of a great marriage. Of course, to be a good conversationalist one needs to be a good listener. We may sometimes find ourselves wondering why the point we are trying to get across to our partner is misunderstood. The underlying problem is that we have lost the art of listening to understand what is being said.

Effective Listening

Effective listening means we are fully present to our partner during conversation. Our very presence invites the intimacy of belonging. A part of us belongs to the other (emotional commitment) and reaches for acceptance in the warmth of our lover's heart. Listening is the most powerful way to show love to our partner because it sends a silent message of caring, respect, and genuine interest in who she is and what she is sharing.

Unquestionably, learning to listen is one of the most difficult exercises in the communication process. To become an effective listener, keep in mind that listening is not a passive act. It's not about just being quiet when our partner is talking but about presence, showing interest in hearing what is being said, without interrupting.

There are a number of ways we can demonstrate to our spouse that we are listening to understand, that we are offering our focused attention. We offer positive feedback by nodding our head in agreement, leaning forward, smiling, and looking in our partner's eyes. From time to time we can say words like "I see", or "I understand", or "I hear you." Try to avoid anticipating the end of your partner's sentence so you can immediately jump in. In other words, don't listen merely to answer, but rather to understand and to empathize.

Listen for ideas, perspectives, feelings, and needs. Hearing what is being said may provide the key to resolving conflict or solving problems. Listen carefully for the unexpressed concerns; take note of how the message is delivered so you can respond appropriately. When you perceive fear offer assurance; if your partner is anxious, offer comfort. Truly sharing hearts and minds with each other provides the glue that cements an enduring relationship.

The Couple's Dialogue

The Couple's Dialogue is a tool for building trust and providing the space for honest, open sharing. It will help you to communicate your point clearly and to be sure that your partner understands what you mean. The Couple's Dialogue is an excellent way to do this. When you express your idea or feeling, use "I" statements; e.g. "I feel hurt when you make decisions without consulting me". The other approach, "You always make decisions without consulting me", puts your partner in the position of having to defend his actions. Ask your partner to repeat back to you what you've said, to paraphrase your statement. Agree to stop after each three or four sentences to give your partner a chance to paraphrase what you've said. Be careful to avoid interpreting or judging what you've heard or offering solutions. The speaker then has a chance to feed back if he has been heard correctly and to clarify feelings, if needed.

Marlene and Dave spent the first few years of their marriage interrupting each other, shouting and accusing but rarely hearing what the other had to say. Their relationship was at a low threshold when they discovered the Couple's Dialogue. It required practice to change the tone of their communication. Gone are the old habits of over-talking each other in an effort to be right, the raised voices, and indignation. This now familiar way of interacting has helped to change the quality of their verbal exchanges. Maybe it can help yours too. The following dialogue illustrates how the couple successfully communicates.

Marlene: "I feel ignored when you constantly change the TV channels without ever asking me what I would like to view."

Dave: "I hear you say you feel ignored when I choose the programming without asking you what you'd like to see."

Marlene: "Yes. I would like the opportunity of handling the remote control so I can choose what I'd like to see. Of course I'd take into account your tastes and preferences."

Dave: "I understand you'd like to have the remote control so you can pick a program that you'd enjoy and you'd inquire if I might enjoy it too. "

Marlene: "I'd appreciate that very much. Do you think we could do this sometimes?"

Dave: "Yes, of course. I was unaware how much I monopolized our choice of viewing. I do like to watch the sports

	events and took it for granted that you enjoyed them too. Is there any particular program that irritates you?"
Marlene:	"I hear you say you were unaware that you made almost all of the choices for our viewing by the holding onto the remote control. And you want to know if any specific program irritates me."
Dave:	"Right. I welcome your input and am willing to relinquish the remote so you can choose what you'd like to see. If there is any program you dislike and I want to see it, can we make some arrangement so both our needs can be met?"
Marlene:	"I like the idea of having access to the remote sometimes but I don't need it all the time. I especially like sitting down with you to watch comedies and the news. Some of the sports interest me and I like to join you for them when I can. And I hear you are willing to work this out."
Dave:	"Thank you for clarifying for me the programs you enjoy watching. I hear loud and clear that you want more sharing of the remote control so you can make choices too."

Since this is an opportunity for mutual sharing and listening, each partner has the chance to express what he/she is feeling and the other partner gets to feed back his/her statements. This is purely a process to understand the other's point of view. If each feels heard, the dialogue is a success. Agree to handle only one issue at a time.

This process is not designed to elicit agreement or create resolution although in some cases it does. Because the subject matter treated here is not complex, Marlene and Dave's conversation could very well continue as follows:

Dave: "Do you have any suggestions for making this work smoother?"

Marlene: "Yes, I think we can work this out if we just leave the remote sitting on the coffee table when the television is switched on. This way we both have access. Will that work for you?"

Dave: "That's a great solution and I may need to be reminded from time to time to put the remote back on the table."

Mastering this technique is well worth the effort and is a very effective way to have clear communication that honors your partner. Being present to your spouse means listening without distractions from television, phones or computers. When either of you has something important to say, make sure it gets priority over any distraction. Sometimes it may be difficult, but keep on listening and really try to understand. Use this feedback process to practice the discipline of effective listening. It will help you to stay present to each other and build honest, open communication in your marriage.

To keep your marriage brimming, with love in the wedding cup,
whenever you're wrong, admit it; whenever you're right, shut up.

OGDEN NASH

Don't Make Assumptions

When we do not communicate clearly or ask for clarification, we often make assumptions. Worse still, we believe our assumptions are correct. Then we defend them even if it means making our partner wrong. Every time we think we know what our partner is thinking or feeling, and don't ask, we are making an assumption. Couples make assumptions about each other's likes and dislikes, needs and wants. Each assumes the other will do what the assumer wants and then is hurt and disappointed when it doesn't happen as expected. This behavior results from the misguided idea that if our partner really loves us, he should know what we want and feel. Trying to read another's mind is hazardous. Forget it! Don't complicate your relationship by falling into the trap of assumption.

Ask for What You Want

One of the cornerstones of a great relationship is the ability to ask for what we want. This presupposes that we are aware of the needs and wants that satisfy us. We have discussed elsewhere the subject of needs and how these differ for men and women.

Taking these differences into account, we need to be clear when we ask. Our partner may have no idea what is most pleasing to us; it is our responsibility to let him know. Learning to ask for what we want could eliminate assumptions, conflict, hurt and the disappointment of unmet expectations.

As a way to express your deeply felt longings, make an agreement with your partner that you will both ask for what you want. With repetition, this agreement will become a habit. Over time it becomes second nature and magically transforms the quality of your togetherness.

Practice the art of asking for what you want so you can experience for yourself a new sense of personal freedom. This is part of the mastery of love, indeed the mastery of life.

Watch Your Words

Consider the fact that there is an inner and an outer aspect to your lives. What causes the pain to either of you in your interaction with each other is not the event that happens or the words carelessly expressed. The problem is not in what transpires but in how you perceive and react to it. Your feelings simply reflect your emotional response to what happened. Always use words that build bridges rather than walls.

Words your partner loves to hear can include:
- I love you.

- You are so kind.
- I'm proud of you.
- I really appreciate you.
- Thank you for doing that.
- I'm listening.
- I'm here for you.
- You have my full attention.
- How are you feeling?
- Please forgive me.
- You are so loving.
- Thank you for sharing.

What counts in making a happy marriage is not so much how compatible you are, but how you deal with incompatibility.

AUTHOR UNKNOWN

Conflict in Relationships

As already discussed, successful couples have about as many disagreements as those couples that crumble under the weight of conflict and eventually divorce.

Successful couples learn how to handle their differences because they have worked at developing skills and attitudes that help them to improve intimacy and strengthen their togetherness. Poor resolution of conflict can contaminate a partnership, whereas good communication and fair fighting can bring partners closer together. Successful couples are invested in building their marriage rather than protecting their egos or winning at all costs.

It may seem easier to avoid conflict altogether – and many couples do. It is worthwhile noting that continuous avoidance of conflict can be a predictor of marriage failure. Paradoxically, the main reason we try not to disagree is the fear of losing each other. Early in the marriage a pattern of avoidance may be established, and for a time it seems to work. Don't be fooled. All the accumulated energy finally erupts and a big blow-up upsets everyone. At this point one or other partner often feels like walking away.

It is comforting to discover that all couples go through a stage of struggle as they learn to adjust to each other. This period can be relatively short and an opportunity for learning more about each other. This is the gift of waking up together, becoming more aware and more conscious of ourselves as individuals and as a couple. Conversely, struggle can pervade the life of the marriage and characterize how the couple 'does relationship'. In other words, they can get stuck in their old patterns unless they are willing to change. Predictably, they persist in behaviors that repeatedly cause disagreement until they get help, go their separate ways, or worse still, settle for a miserable life together. In this style of relating the sense of belonging is diminished, the heart closes down and something very precious is lost.

The way out of this dilemma and the key to growing the

relationship is self-realization. When people are willing to confront their inner dialogue – their story about how and why life and their partner are a certain way – they will find the truth and feel a sense of freedom. In the light of this truth we must be willing to change so we can continue to live freely. If the first priority is to grow the marriage, spouses will be willing to embrace change and negotiate new ways of being together. These skills can be learned. There may still be areas where partners agree to disagree but eliminate the destructive behaviors that cause massive withdrawals of energy from the marriage. We can learn how to disagree and still keep our love alive, grow our marriage and build intimacy. This realization will prove to be a bridge from the tyranny of the past to the joy of each present moment.

Fear of conflict is the villain, not conflict itself. Once the partners learn to probe their stories, and agree to stop fighting the reality of them, the fear of conflict will dissipate and will be a useful tool for working through differences. The goal here is to preserve the integrity of the marriage and to sustain or, when needed, restore mutual love.

Anatomy of a Fight

Marcie and Rob both held senior positions in their respective companies. They had busy schedules that resulted in their spending very little time together. Eager to advance in their careers, they accepted the time apart, but after several months Marcie began to resent it. She initially accused her husband of ignoring her. He felt guilty but stayed silent. She attempted to make more demands on his time, voicing the need for home decorating, but he was deaf to her pleas. Rob came home later and later – usually stopping at the gym - to avoid his wife's demands. When her requests went unanswered, she pressured him some more. This distressed husband found the peace of his den very inviting and spent more and more time there.

Finally, Marcie angrily accused her husband of abandoning her, called him disparaging names and blamed him for everything that was wrong in her life. Given her long litany of grievances, it seemed he could do nothing right.

Rob had some grievances too. In his own sarcastic way he let his wife know he was not thrilled with the way she looked (a little plumper than on their wedding day), the way she took him for granted and the way she disrespected him in front of their friends. They were both fully engaged in a 'no-win' argument. Each tried to hold their ground thinking the other was insensitive. They felt truly pained from this exchange and wondered where their love had gone. Anxious to resolve their differences and to improve their marriage, they asked for help.

He confessed he did not understand how much Marcie missed his company and the opportunity for sharing and meaningful conversation. Nor did he realize that she, like most women, needed her quota of affection and he was not around to give it. Slowly he began to sense the reason for her growing resentment.

Marcie was oblivious to the fact that she could have asked for more time, conversation and affection. It became clear to her that she assumed that her husband should know what she wanted. She was receptive to the idea that the more she demanded and pressured him, the more he wanted to retreat. Now she could grasp why he came home later and spent time in the den. He, in turn, accepted responsibility for escaping rather than facing and dealing with his wife's requests.

Marcie recognized that she had resorted to food to satisfy her feelings of aloneness and wasn't happy with the extra pounds. She was unaware that her physical attractiveness was very important to her partner. He finally asked her to refrain from making remarks that exposed his shortcomings and diminished him in the eyes of his friends. She agreed and admitted that she had done this unconsciously never realizing how much he treasured her admiration of him.

The stuck place for both of them, as for many couples, was their sense of disappointment with their partner. We all experience this from time to time, only because we have expectations of how the other should be. We have such a tendency to project our disappointments and missed expectations on our partner. In time, we all come to learn that when we are upset about our own thinking we are upset with our partner's thinking too. And we find ways to let them know! Paradoxically, when we are at peace with our inner world of thought, we are more at peace with our lover's. So any time you catch yourself blaming him/her for your problems, stop and revise your thought process. You are responsible for your thoughts and only you can change them. When you check your inner conversation, you will discover that he/she is not the problem; it's the story you have created around that person that is causing your suffering.

Rob and Marcie's sharing opened up huge possibilities for working together to accommodate each other's needs and grow their love and caring for each other. It took them only a short time to master the skills of heartfelt listening and honest disclosure. Over time, they learned to ask for what they wanted. This helped build trust and safety between them. When they felt their emotions building up, they made agreements about setting a time to meet and talk things over. Because their greatest concern was to preserve their love and care for each other, they considered their problems a wake up call to a more vibrant life together.

Our experience has taught us that when couples are willing to face the truth of who they are and take ownership of it, (wake up together) they accelerate their marriage intimacy, decelerate their arguments and increase their chances for a successful marriage.

Reminders

- Your first priority is to safeguard your marriage.
- Use the Couple's Dialogue – "I" statements only.

- Listen to understand.
- Be aware of non-verbal cues.
- Maintain caring and mutual respect.
- Discuss only the issue at hand – no resurrecting the past.
- No shaming, blaming, yelling or name-calling.
- If tempers flare, agree to a time out.
- Don't make assumptions.
- Listen to discover unmet needs.
- Speak the words your partner loves to hear.
- Ask for what you want.
- Be willing to confront your old ideas and adopt new ones.
- Make new agreements for sharing and disclosure.
- Use conflict to get to know each other better.

The Best Part – Making Up

Disagreements are inevitable; making up is imperative. Willingness to build a bridge to your partner and attempts to repair the breach are essential to restore loving feelings. Couples who habitually reach out to each other in a gesture of conciliation grow stronger marriages and report deeper levels of happiness.

When we feel alienated from each other, we want to make up – find our way back into each other's heart. Part of making up is being able to handle those leftover feelings. Even when the war of words is over, there often are leftover feelings of hurt, resentment or confusion that express in a cool, standoffish uneasiness between the couple. She may feel sad that he's still closed down and not connecting. He may be nervous that she'll ridicule him. He may wish she'd make eye contact, smile and somehow make it easier for him to find his way back into her heart. Each waits for the other to reach out, make a loving gesture and restore that loving connection. Humor can be a very effective way of reaching out to your partner.

Magic Words for Restoring the Heart Connection

- I'm sorry I hurt you.
- Please forgive me.
- I forgive you.
- I didn't mean to hurt you, can you forgive me?
- I love you; can we put this behind us?
- I apologize for the hurtful things I said.
- What can I do to help us get back our loving feelings?
- It wasn't your entire fault.
- I too said some things I didn't mean.
- I want you to know that even though I got mad, I still love you.
- I see the truth of what you said, and I'm willing to own that.

It is not the lack of love,
but a lack of friendship that makes unhappy marriages.
FRIEDRICH NIETZSCHE

Forgiveness is a healing balm for the soul. It means we are ready to let go of the hurt and drop the old story rather than saving it for the next disagreement. It sends a message that we take responsibility for what happened between us rather than blame the other. Forgiveness builds a bridge to the heart of our spouse. It allows us to remove the protective armor we put around our hearts to avoid getting hurt again. The act of forgiveness opens us up so love can easily flow between us. Offer it freely and accept it graciously. And reap the rewards of deepened intimacy.

Lovers' Insights

- Encouraging, loving words are energy gainers.
- Destructive comments are energy drainers.
- Forgive mistakes and ask for forgiveness when you need to.
- Get honest with yourself about your story and stop denying reality.
- Build bridges to each other and keep love flowing.

We have found that open, honest communication is key to the success of committed relationship. Taking the time to practice new ways of sharing thoughts and feelings promotes healthy togetherness. Cultivating attitudes of careful listening allows us to be present to issues and open to change. Marriage is a joint venture, an opportunity to grow and deepen intimacy with one another. It's not too late to kindle or rekindle the open, sharing type of relationship you've always wanted. Conflict can come and go without impacting you negatively; in fact, it can be turned around to become your ally in mutual growth. Realizing the truth of your own past and your aspirations for the future frees you into the present moment to fully enjoy the love you share.

CHAPTER 7

Cultivating Stress Awareness

~~~~~~~

Learning to listen to your own body is vital
to improving your health and the quality of your life.

JON KABAT-ZINN

Many of the roles we assume in our relationship carry the potential for unleashing stressful emotional baggage. Today, more couples are working, sharing domestic responsibilities and feeling overwhelmed and stressed. Reaching deeper into ourselves can best ease the pain and inner turbulence that arise from the busyness of life and societal expectations. Our heart knows the inevitability of human suffering, and has the wisdom to ease its distress and soothe its weariness. Here we offer a sampling of ways to reconnect with our deeper core and rejuvenate our spirit.

Stress

However long we live, we will experience stress. It is an inevitable part of life. Stress is our reaction to any change to which we must adapt. Our resistance to the reality of what is happening prevents us from making the adjustment or correction that will allow us to live in peace. Possibilities run the gamut from real physical danger to the euphoria of falling in love. As a couple, you experience a myriad of daily events that have the potential for minor or major stress. How you respond to life's challenges and excitement determines the effect these events will have on your sense of well-being.

Stressful, painful experiences are not caused by what anyone else has done or by any event. Stress is the result of what you tell yourself about what happened. Don't rush to blame your partner or your circumstances. Better direct your questions inwardly and discover what struck such a deep chord in you and initiated your reaction. Your questions have to be of self-inquiry that will lead to greater self-awareness. You have within you a power that is greater than any uneasy situation your life or relationship can present, but you have to become aware of the power before you can use it.

This power is our world of thoughts and feelings. Here we experience all that happens around us and in our marriage. From this inner world we see the world of our relationship, so, in truth, the inner determines the outer. Our inner view of life determines the outer, not the other way around. The breakdowns in relationships that occur are real stressors – loss of belonging hurts us deeply. Working through the pain of loss becomes a catalyst for superb breakthroughs in personal and soul growth. So when up against an obstacle in marriage, we have not encountered something that destroys our happiness; we have simply come face to face with our current level of awareness. Our partner is not the cause of our stress or unhappiness; these feelings come from deep within us.

With self-discovery you gain freedom from much of the pain and stress that unconscious marriages experience. Every time you become more aware of the real cause of your unhappiness and stress, you grow more towards wholeness and true happiness. You no longer have to suffer mentally or emotionally when you come to understand that you have power over your inner world.

How we hold the world in our eye and
heart is what we and the world will become.

JACK KORNFIELD

Stress is often the result of, or pained response to loss of employment, family, business, husband/wife, parent, child, property or reputation. Loss of love, whether through death or alienation, leaves emptiness in the heart that wounds us deeply. The sense of grief can feel overwhelming – grief for the feeling of loss and the erosion of one's sense of identity. The sense of belonging has been ruptured and the heart has a profound need for contact. But the threads of connection have become invisible. And yet your heart is the fortress around the rich resources that lie dormant deep within you. The heart, broken open by tragedy or loss, knows how to balance vulnerability with strength. A broken heart is a magnet for receptivity and compassion, healing and new beginnings. As the seer tells us, *the worst of times can become the best of times; the lesser often gives way to the greater.* So take courage when you suffer reversals; there is healing, and life still has purpose. Profound loss can pierce the veil of unconscious living and reveal a deep sense of connection to our spiritual self – the reality of life lived with greater awareness.

Stress Reliever #1: Self Observation

One of the great transformational techniques for relieving tension is self-observation. Watch yourself in your interactions with your partner. Observe how you respond and how you listen. Become aware of how you talk to yourself during your relationship experiences. Although you are now living with that special partner, in truth most of your living is done within your inner conversation – you live in and act from your inner dialogue with yourself. Start observing your self-talk – without any judgment or criticism. What do you say when you talk to yourself? What are you telling yourself about the challenges in your relationship? Repeated thoughts and feelings crystallize into beliefs that, in turn, dictate behavior.

Stress Reliever #2: Mindfulness

Mindfulness is a way of paying attention to our inner thoughts. We do this to better understand ourselves and to restore calm to our busy, anxious mind. It's about living in the now with a sense of peaceful serenity. This technique has been in existence for over 2,500 years, is simple to practice and can be done anywhere. However, even with our best intention to slow down, our thoughts continue to race. It takes a little practice to switch from reacting and general busyness to taming our inner chatter and feeling calm and relaxed. An easy way to relax is with mindfulness meditation. To be mindful is to be aware of our bodies, to be in touch with our emotions and open to our intuition.

Sitting in mindfulness, both our bodies and minds can be at peace and totally relaxed... one is not only restful and happy, but alert and awake. Meditation is not evasion; it is a serene encounter with reality.

THICH NHAT HANH

The key to mindfulness is focus on the breath. Practice this easy exercise by sitting comfortably in a quiet place, eyes closed and simply paying attention to your breathing. Start by taking a deep breath; breathe from deep down in your diaphragm. As you breathe out, feel the tension leave your body. After several breaths you will experience a mild sense of relaxation.

When your mind wanders away from your breathing – as it inevitably will – simply bring it back and focus again on your breathing. Whether you spend five or thirty-five minutes, you'll benefit from the relaxed alert feeling when you close out your meditation and return to your regular routine. Don't be surprised if you have more distractions than focused breathing during the first few sessions. With practice, you will master this ancient relaxation technique. You will want to return to it because of the calm serene feelings it promotes.

Serious practitioners of mindfulness continue to cultivate daily use because of its other beneficial effects. The very act of disciplining one's thoughts creates opportunities for strengthening inner resources that help to combat stress and promote peace of mind. These resources include: patience, seeing things through new eyes, trust, acceptance, non-judging, non-efforting and the ability to let go and stop worrying. These are resources that can enhance everyone's life. In the context of relationship, mindfulness means being fully present and fully receptive to the totality of one's partner.

Stress Reliever #3: Walking Meditation

Mindfulness can also be practiced as a walking meditation. You simply are in the moment being aware of every step you take and the sensations in your body as you do so. It is so refreshing to take a walking meditation and get in tune with the beauty of creation; notice the exquisite detail of flowers, trees, butterflies, clouds, frost patterns and the multiplicity of nature's bounty. Even a ten-minute walk will refresh your mind and give that relaxed renewed feeling. You are then ready to face any situation from a place of renewed strength and vitality with a feeling that nothing could disturb the calm peace of your soul. Walking meditation is always done in silence. You can do it alone or with your partner.

Universal Stressors

Stress is an inherent part of living and can be triggered in relationship by any of the following:

- Money
- Buying or selling a home
- Parenting
- Sex
- Dual careers
- Conflict arising from poor communication
- Divorce
- Chronic illness or accident
- Loneliness
- Grief or loss
- Work
- Meeting deadlines

Stress is not limited to those situations, as you have probably experienced in your own circumstances. The human condition itself is fraught with stress possibilities. How you cope with life and minimize or manage stressful reactions is key to your health, happiness and longevity. Make a decision to deepen (or initiate) your relationship with your heart wisdom. Scientists tell us that a heart knows its need for love and compassion, belonging and a sense of the spiritual. So we are never alone – the intelligence of the heart is ever vigilant and invites us into the warmth and security of its caring.

More Stress Relief

Guided Meditation: This is a meditation technique where you are guided to simply survey your inner landscape. Create a setting in your mind that feels peaceful. This is a function of your inner creativity to orchestrate a pleasing, relaxing experience. You may choose to use this time to connect with your inner self, ask for guidance or resolve a problem.

If your intention is to use this time to ask for guidance, direction or healing, spend a few minutes in total silence. After this period of silence, you may be guided to offer a few words of gratitude and then be reoriented to your physical surroundings. It helps to have soft non-intrusive music in the background. Some people prefer this type of meditation. Done daily, it helps to cultivate a serene, peaceful state of mind. Audiotapes and compact discs exist to help you reflect on a variety of life situations.

No matter what is happening in your relationship, you will always return from meditation more relaxed, with a clearer perspective and better able to handle life's challenges.

Body Scan: This is an excellent method for relaxing and relieving stress any time. We find it particularly helpful after a full day of mental concentration. (It's a way to get out of your head and into your body). It is also helpful if you are feeling physical pain or fatigue. Simply lie down, loosen your clothing for comfort, with hands by your side, legs slightly spread. Eyes closed, direct your inner attention to your left foot as though you were checking it out for comfort level. Focus consecutively on your toes, arch, top of your foot, heel, and ankle being aware of the various functions each part performs and how well they serve you. Continue focusing on your leg, calf, knee joint with all its intricacies and flexibility, thigh and hip.

Switch your attention now to your right foot and proceed in the same manner to your right hip. Shift attention now to your lower back, pelvis, abdomen, stomach and chest. Don't forget to focus on the various organs – heart, lungs, kidneys and liver. And keep moving up through your body to your neck and shoulders, often the place where you hold tension.

The other places that likely feel tight are your scalp, forehead, cheeks, mouth and jaw. Try to stay alert long enough to visit your head area since it needs the most attention after a long day.

If you plan to do the body scan after you get home at the end of the day and before dinner, be sure to alert your partner. Chances are that you will feel so relaxed that you will gently drift off to sleep – and maybe miss dinner!

Relief from Insomnia: Autogenic Relaxation.

Researchers have found that it is natural for us upon falling asleep to feel slightly warm and to experience feelings of heaviness. When we have trouble dropping off to sleep, our mind races, we get fidgety and very likely disturb our partner. At those times, we can help ourselves to fall asleep by mimicking the body's natural patterns of warmth and heaviness.

This is very simple. Lie on your back, arms by your side, legs slightly apart. Eyes closed, shift your attention to your right arm and say silently and slowly: "My right arm is warm and heavy. Repeat. "My left arm is warm and heavy". Repeat. "Both arms are warm and heavy". Do the same for your right leg, left leg, and then both legs. Shift attention to your lower back. "My lower back is warm and heavy". Repeat, and so on for your abdomen, solar plexus, center back, chest, upper back and shoulders. If you have not fallen asleep by now, continue to the back of your neck, scalp, forehead, cheeks, jaw and neck. You will rarely ever complete the whole exercise before sleep takes you into its magic adventure. Your partner will thank you for your relaxed bedtime ritual and you will appreciate the ease of falling asleep naturally. It is also helpful to lull you back to sleep if you wake up during the night.

Other De-Stressing Techniques

Sometimes, when stressful thoughts creep into your mind during the day, it's useful to have some affirming or coping statements. Wherever you are, it only takes a second to remind yourself, '*No matter what happens, I can handle it.*' Or, '*I can relax now and take care of this later.*' That gives you an opportunity to calm down in the moment and not make any decision until you've had time to strategize or talk it over with your partner. When you and your partner disagree and feelings are running high, remind yourself '*Regardless of all that's been said, we still love one another.*'

Tensions and conflicting needs and views are an integral part of any committed relationship. Possibilities for stress arise in situations related to in-laws, work, scheduling, family events, sickness, unemployment, children and a host of other eventualities. Learning to discipline oneself through the use of any of the practices mentioned, or any form of physical exercise, will release the pent up stress. It helps to agree on an area of the house where you can go to be alone while you de-stress. Any safety valve is helpful. Some couples find lovemaking to be their favorite de-stressor. Few would argue with that!

Marriage is not a solution to your problems. In life we all face challenges. Problems come disguised as the building blocks of personal and relationship growth. You'd rather not have them, but you will. The good news is that they get easier and easier to manage. Problems are solved when you employ the techniques to handle them.

Reduce Stress by Solving Problems Together

Take some time together to look at issues objectively. Know that the challenges are not unique to you and that they have a solution. Enlist the help of your partner to solve the problem. Equipped with paper and pen, write your major challenge, stating it quite simply in a sentence or two. On page two write your second problem. If you have multiple problems, keep writing them at the top of separate sheets of paper. Make sure to write down anything that concerns you.

When you have listed each problem on a separate page, go back to page one and read the statement about your main problem. Now relax into your imagination, your creative power, where the truth of the situation resides. Allow solutions to enter your minds. Don't discount any thoughts. Now take turns listing all the possible solutions that arise in your minds. Continue to allow your imagination to create possible solutions and note them all.

If some of your ideas seem impractical, write them down anyway. Try to stay focused on what is real and present. Putting ideas on paper can inspire you towards the best solution. Affirm that you are being guided to the best answer. Out of this process and the ensuing dialogue, the best resolution will evolve. Staying in the reality of a situation will always guide you home because you cannot find truth while resisting reality. Being present to *what is* means you are available to all possibilities. Allow yourselves to question each possible resolution; 'Is this true and is it real for us?' Apply the same techniques to each individual problem and allow outcomes to unfold.

The benefits of this process are that you clearly agree upon a definition of your problems and you only focus on what is real. Carrying problems in your head often causes unnecessary suffering. Challenges are rarely resolved in this way and can cause both partners avoidable stress. Committing problems to paper and honestly confronting them is a great stress remover. It works! Just remember to bring a positive attitude to the problem solving process.

Reducing stress through mindfulness practice is a valuable tool for anyone who is committed to walk the path of awareness and personal transformation.

CHAPTER 8

Taking Care of Business

The courses of true love never did run smooth.

WILLIAM SHAKESPEARE

Money is one of the biggest issues that challenge couples. There is no doubt; money can have a major impact on your relationship. It's common knowledge that financial concerns can spark problems in marriage; in fact, many surveys show that unresolved conflicts concerning money are the most common cause of divorce. The troubles usually spring from the couple's differing values around money. One may put a higher priority on saving while the other prefers to spend or, value owning a home while the other may want to travel or finance a business. These unresolved differences hang around like a shadow and sap energy from an otherwise good relationship.

The ability to handle money agreeably is an important skill that adds strength to a successful marriage. Though your roles may change over the years, you will continue to be partners in financial decision-making and fiscal responsibility. Individuals relate to money in different ways due to the unique influences in their lives and so make financial decisions based on their perceptions of money. Differing influences aside, financial bliss is possible when you develop an understanding of how money works.

Let's begin by examining how you handle money in your relationship.

- How well do you understand each other's priorities about money?
- Do you make decisions about finances (especially major purchases) individually or jointly?
- Have you defined the quality of life you both aspire to financially?
- Have you set financial goals for your lives together?
- Do you talk openly and regularly about money issues rather than wait for a crisis?
- Or, is money a subject you would rather not discuss?
- How important is financial security to you?
- Do you have an emergency account?
- Do you make impromptu decisions to spend?
- How much, if any, credit card debt do you have?
- Does one or both of you create income?
- How much do you save?

It's important to make agreements early in your relationship concerning all of the above questions. Prior to marriage you made financial decisions for yourself. Now the decisions involve your spouse and you may not have all the best answers for handling your joint finances. The solutions to your financial challenges do not always come easily, but having agreements with your partner on how to approach each situation will bring peace of mind to both of you. In money matters, it's imperative that you let each other know about your individual needs and desires and that you clearly understand the other's priorities. Consider having an agreement as to what constitutes a major purchase. At what level is it appropriate to consult with your partner before making such a purchase? Agreements go a long way to eliminating the conflict that can arise if one partner comes home with an unexpected major item and the other is concerned about the mortgage payment.

If you differ in major ways in terms of financial priorities or spending habits and cannot reach satisfactory agreement, consider consulting with a competent financial professional.

Organize a specific time for a short meeting each week to review financial matters together and ensure you are in agreement when it comes to your money. This means you won't have to spend fun or leisure time discussing money concerns. The two of you working collaboratively will build up your financial resources faster than one doing it alone.

The Heart of the Matter

To be successful in money matters it is wise to develop a joint strategy for managing your financial affairs. Combine this with a right attitude and determination and you develop a formula for success. You cannot choose not to give attention to money matters because ignoring this area of your lives could result in frustrating and painful experiences accompanied by inevitable conflict.

Like most couples, we made our share of mistakes until we decided to educate ourselves. Of the many books we read, four were particularly helpful:

1. *Seven Strategies for Wealth and Happiness, by Jim Rohn*
   This book paints a broad picture of some common sense and disciplined approaches to managing money for the short and long term. Very practical and often amusing.

2. *The Wealthy Barber, by David Chilton*
   A great story, simply written, and full of helpful advice for anyone planning their financial future. The barber truly understands all the money basics any family needs and coaches his small group effectively.

3. *Rich Dad, Poor Dad, by Guy Kiyosaki*
   The author conveys his financial wisdom through the story of his own learning about money. He compares and contrasts his own father with his friend's father. Their respective monetary philosophies read like a dictionary of do's and dont's. The reader can easily discern what works well and what to avoid.

4. *The 9 Steps to Financial Freedom, by Suze Orman*
   This book goes beyond the nuts and bolts of money management.

The author successfully explores the psychological and spiritual power money has in our lives. She offers expert advice on how to let go of the influences that keep us from the experience of true prosperity.

It's really simple! The quality of your financial life is determined by the difference between your income and your expenses. The more you save and the less you spend, the higher your quality of life. The challenge for all couples is to move past the zone of instant gratification. The fact that your money is so easily accessible through electronic banking can be convenient, but it can also be a trap. Instant access to money often leads to out of control spending. Quick access to your money works well when you are making on-line purchases or rushing through the checkout at the store; but when this instant money mindset is applied to your finances in general, you could be buying problems!

Becoming financially secure is not about the size of your household income but the wisdom you apply in distributing your earnings. You can have a marriage where you both enjoy the comfort of worry-free finances if you are willing to master some simple yet powerful ideas about how money works. The majority of couples derive their income from two main sources. The first is compensation from a salaried position, an entrepreneurial business or a profession. This likely represents the bulk of their income. Most of us will reach a point when, no matter how much we love our work, we'll decide to downsize our working hours or discontinue completely. This is what our society calls retirement.

Your other source of income is derived from the return on your investments. The amount depends on how well your money is working for you. If you turn a percentage of your income into maturing investments, there will likely come a time when your investments are adequate to take care of your lifestyle and you no longer need to work. Careful preparation and diligent attention eventually results in the rewarding stage known as financial independence. At this point, you can choose to stop working and let your money continue to work for you.

The Best Solution – Take Control of Your Money!

Don't ask yourself what the world needs –
ask yourself what makes you come alive, and then go do it. Because
what the world needs is people who have come alive.

HAROLD THURMAN WHITMAN

If you want to avoid money problems in your marriage, agree to take control of your finances now. Taking control means that you move from struggling unconsciously with money to becoming conscious of the fact that all the decisions are in your hands. You are the ones who will solve your financial challenges and build financial security – not your job, your family or anyone in the world around you! You alone hold the key to the solution.

Learn how to make the wisest and best decisions about your money. A word of caution: Banks and other institutions may give you helpful ideas on how to manage your money, but remember it's your money and these organizations often sell you the products that benefit them most. Don't depend on any outside factors to make the decisions for you – equip yourselves with the tools to establish and control your financial independence!

Where Do You Start?

First, make an agreement that you want to take control of your finances and create financial security. As long as you procrastinate, financial struggle is inevitable. The unhappy consequence: many of your dreams will remain only dreams never to be realized.

Financially speaking, couples go through a learning period and an earning period. Basically your first 25 years are for learning the rudiments of money management and the subsequent forty years is your earning period. Depending on how well you manage these two periods, when your earning days are complete, you will either be financially secure or dependent on outside help to see you through your retirement years.

Building Financial Security

- Agree to be selfish where your money is concerned, by putting yourselves first. Consider that paying yourselves first is part of your monthly financial obligations and put it at the top of your list. Always! This is ancient wisdom that works! Live on 70% (or less) of your joint income and start a savings program with the rest.

- Before beginning your long term saving plan make a goal to set aside the equivalent of three months income in a savings account that you use only for a *real emergency*. This is *not* vacation money – it is security and peace of mind money to handle those unexpected emergencies. Make sure it is easily accessible. Make an agreement that you do not touch this account or the interest it yields. This provision will reduce financial stress in your marriage.

- Start a long-term savings or investment program that works for you and begin it now! The earlier you begin, the more your money will compound. Congratulations! Your Financial Independence Account will make a huge difference to your futures!

The most insidious and dangerous financial challenge is the horrible disease of DEBT! Over-spending with credit cards or installment loans is dangerous to the health of your wallet and your relationship. Beware! Too many marriages have floundered on the rocks of plastic.

Looking Into the Future

Retirement may seem distant for you now. However, be aware that the money habits you develop in your early years together will have a huge impact on the quality of your lives in later years. Time will pass and retirement will come. Take some simple steps now so you will be ready. Don't wait to start building towards financial independence. Imagine the peace of mind you'll have if you give just a little thought to this distant subject now. With desire, discipline and some knowledge, you can make a huge difference to your cash accumulation at retirement. Almost 70% of the population makes no plans for their retirement. Be wise – make sure you are in the 30% that do!

The solution to creating financial serenity in your marriage is to make informed choices and take control of your financial lives together. It's about putting your lives and your marriage on the road to financial security.

Practice cutting expenses when you can, find the best value when you buy, and refuse to pay too much. Avoid the buy now, pay later syndrome and always ask yourself when you go to buy something, 'Is it a need or a want?' Be totally honest with yourself and each other and you will reach your goals. Now that you are more aware, your financial future doesn't have to be in question. Have fun in your weekly financial meetings; agree to control what you can, to set financial goals and to become financially successful. Then you can really dream and make your dreams come true!

CHAPTER 9

Intentional Intimacy

~~~~~

Romantic love is a passionate spiritual emotional-sexual attachment
between a man and a woman that reflects
a high regard for the value of each other's person.

NATHANIEL BRANDEN

Sexual intimacy embraces the total experience of love shared between emotionally committed partners. Sex is one of the most powerful drives in human beings. Nature created it that way so we could fulfill our longing to be connected and feel complete. Heart-centered intimate relationship was designed to be pleasurable. Eros seduces us into the enjoyment of sex as a way to complete each other physically, mentally, emotionally and spiritually. The seduction of being so fully present to each other opens the door to completion and belonging. The ultimate gift of sexual energy is to make your lover feel irresistibly attractive, sensual and desirable.

Sexual intimacy between committed partners has a very different quality from casual sex. The former is a pleasurable union of body, mind and soul. The latter affords us physical gratification and varying degrees of pleasure, but it lacks depth and meaning. The biological urge may be relieved but is rarely satiated because the need for belonging and heartfelt connection is wanting. Casual sexual relations occur between two personalities who think they have something to gain from each other.

In intimate relationship, sexual feelings color all aspects of the couple's togetherness. Wholesome marriages bear the hallmark of joy, pleasantness and that scarcely definable something that tells the world the couple is committed, happy and solid together. There is an energy that flows easily between them, an intimacy that speaks of the sacredness of their unique coupling. This is the mysterious attractiveness that exudes from a relationship sealed in sexual fulfillment.

Rodin, the French sculptor, captured an exquisite sense of intimate touch in his renowned sculpture titled *The Kiss*. We had the pleasure of viewing this magnificently crafted piece housed in the Rodin Museum in Paris. The sculptor finely crafted two bodies in an intimate embrace about to kiss. We marveled at the sensitivity of this loving gesture; two lovers, sensually drawn to each other, enchanted by a magic moment beyond time and space. The beauty of the piece clearly demonstrates how much our sense of touch connects us to each other in very intimate ways.

People marry for a variety of reasons, sexual fulfillment being high on the list. Where there is an unrestricted sharing of hearts, couples can satisfy their need for emotional closeness, deepening intimacy and pure pleasure. Satisfying sex is delicious; it feeds love, promotes emotional togetherness and connects us to one another at a deeply satisfying level. The fusion of body, mind and heart lifts us momentarily beyond our human aloneness into a timeless cosmic unity. This opportunity to trust oneself fully to another is embraced and nurtured in the context of a heart-centered marriage.

Sex fulfills different purposes in marriage. It is one of the ways we communicate our deepest feelings of affection for each other. Sexual satisfaction expands the more you get to know your lover and allow your lover to know you. Take the time to share desires and expectations as well as concerns with your lover long before lovemaking. Talk about what you want, express your willingness to experiment. In their shared, intimate, private moments great lovers learn together how to enhance the pleasures of mutually satisfying sex. Cultivate the art of lovemaking. Spontaneity, playfulness and lusty experimentation add depth, intensity and passion to your relationship. This is why it is so important to protect your alone time. Committed lovers, let nothing take priority over your adult playtime. Cherish those moments; it's the time you build trust and deepen intimacy.

True intimacy is a reflection of the degree of mutual need-satisfaction experienced by both partners. Every sexual encounter doesn't have to be fireworks – and probably won't. Like most things in life, sexual desire and frequency has its ebbs and flows. In the early stages of relationship, sexual encounters have the sizzle of newness and delight. But they lack emotional depth because we do not yet really know each other. Over time, the deep bonding that flows from repeated acts of love shared and needs communicated ripens into its unique fragrance of intimacy.

Even the richest relationships can be sidelined by the incursions of work and family obligations. Varying work schedules, dual careers and parenting are demanding and can draw energy from a couple's private time. Avoid the trap of being so invested in becoming good parents and providers that your relationship takes a back seat. It is all too easy to take each other for granted as you move through the daily routine of careers, parenthood and household responsibilities. Never pass up the chance for erotic pleasure and mutual tenderness.

Honest, open communication kindles the fire of sexual intimacy and fuels the flames of love throughout your relationship. Sex is one of the ways you communicate your deepest feelings for your lover. Talk straight to your partner about your expectations and desires; talk about your need for togetherness, your aching for the touch and warmth of physical contact. The more you understand and interpret each other's sexual passions, the deeper will be your mutual satisfaction. Discuss the ways you wish to engage your partner; agree on the roles you are willing to play and be open to reverse them when the situation arises. Approach lovemaking as an exquisite art form: practice often and refine your skills.

The Intimacy of Affection

We are all angels with one wing. We fly only when we embrace.

LEO BUSCAGLIA

Affection is one of the powerful and meaningful ways lovers communicate their love and caring for each other. Affection is captured in gestures that secretly convey messages that your lover finds you attractive, gorgeous, and titillating. The lovers' intimate expressions of caring can happen anytime anywhere. Tokens of affection exchanged between couples serves to nurture the love and caring they feel for each other. Women thrive on affection. They relish hugging, hand holding, sensual smiles that say, '*I only have eyes for you.*' Ask any woman how she feels when she receives a bouquet of flowers or her favorite chocolates from her lover. Watch how her composure changes when she reads a card or love note from the most important person in her life. Intimate candlelight dinners together evoke the same delight. The very way she prepares for special events speaks volumes about her fascination that he finds her irresistible and makes her important in his life.

Wives interpret their husband's affectionate gestures as messages of care and protection – that assurance that he will always be there for her. This bonds her heart more deeply to his.

Husbands also appreciate affectionate gestures although they may respond to them differently. He often interprets affection as her way of caring for him. And just for the record, he also loves to find a love coupon for a date. Thrill him with a mushy love note or card on his pillow or in his travel bag.

Romance flows from the heart, the nurturing place that allows love and passion to flourish. So be creative in how you express your love. A great romantic encounter is often conceived very early in the day. Don't ever be concerned that your early morning planning will get in the way of spontaneity; on the contrary, the anticipation builds, creative ideas expand throughout the day, and then the magic, the ethereal fusion of heart, mind and body in those emotionally charged moments of passion, confirms that the joy of sexual intimacy is its own gratifying reward.

Rituals for Lovers

- Kiss, cuddle and affirm your love even before you leave your bed in the morning.
- Have breakfast together, if possible.
- Check in during the day by phone or email.
- Surprise him/her occasionally with flowers, a book or chocolates, theater tickets, or sports event reservations.
- Remember birthdays, anniversaries and dates that are especially important to your relationship. Celebrate them with lovingly selected gifts, mementoes or events that have a romantic flavor.
- Call at the end of your day to reconnect and let him/her know your anticipated arrival time.
- Always kiss hello and goodbye.
- Close out the day with a loving embrace and whatever feels natural.

One couple's sharing of their favorite connecting ritual:

Our special ritual for connecting emotionally is to offer each other a body massage. Firstly, it helps us to relax and the sensual body stroking is the magic touch we both enjoy as a prelude to intimacy. Sometimes we share how much our relationship gives joy to our lives, but often the massage is like a deep silent ritual of arousal. At that point, our hearts, minds and bodies are totally open to each other and the rest is the secret that remains between lovers.

Lovers' Reminders

- Look at him with adoring eyes or stroke his hair gently; he will love it and probably interpret it as an invitation for sex.
- Create the environment that clearly says, 'I love you, let's share this love nest and let's build a great life together.'
- Give her your undivided attention; talk, laugh, share, enjoy each other's company.
- Help him to understand your need for affection and how his spontaneous gestures draw you closer to his heart and make him irresistible.
- Ask him to share his hopes and dreams – encourage and support him to pursue them – and then do it!
- Communicate your deepest longings by opening your heart to her – and then listen to embrace hers.

Enduring Intimacy

Nothing could be more satisfying than a robust, passionate love affair that mellows over the years. The early romantic phase of the relationship brings its own dizzying delight and although, in time, the bloom fades on the rose, the tree grows stronger every year. Never lose the thrill of giving your hearts into each other's keeping. Those moments of total oblivion when your hearts are tenderly given and shared are the elixir of enduring intimacy. Romance continues to add its undeniable brush strokes to the colored canvas of your togetherness. Over time, you will feel a deepening sense of belonging as you continue to offer shelter and comfort in each other's hearts.

Sexual intimacy that is cultivated in the early years of marriage, watered and carefully tended through the years of raising children, will remain strong in the middle and later years. Alfred Charles Kinsey, a sociologist, interviewed close to 20,000 people regarding their sexual habits. The Kinsey report defied conventional wisdom (sexual intimacy declines with age) by announcing that a greater percentage of married couples enjoyed increasing physical intimacy with each passing decade. Mature love can be as delicious and sensually satisfying as any courtship experience.

Sexual Intimacy – the Explosive Phenomenon

Nature has graciously reserved a most savory delight for those couples that have consistently attended to the fires of passion throughout the years of their togetherness. It is an electrifying experience. (Reread: A Lover's Invitation at the opening of this book). What could be more seductive and enticing than to be transported beyond space and time in the erotic embrace of your lover? In this ethereal moment, reality ceases; two hearts fuse into one. Floating in a sea of eternal pleasure, all longing is fulfilled. The fantasy of love's perfect dream takes you to other worlds where all is new. In the magic of pure enchantment you see infinity in the eyes of your lover. The view transcends age and circumstance. Together you drink the sweet nectar of passionate love from the cup of bliss. Your hearts are forever bonded; your lover is both within you and beside you. This peak experience of emotional oneness transcends all others. Enjoy!

Reflections

- Honest, open communication kindles the fire of sexual intimacy and fuels the flames throughout your relationship.
- Talk straight to your lover about your expectations and desires regarding lovemaking.
- Great sex happens when you are willing to experiment and learn together how to pleasure each other.
- Set priorities so hectic schedules and family responsibilities don't intrude on your intimate time.

- Hugs, kisses, sensual glances, and affectionate gestures shared throughout the day are all preludes to romantic time together.
- Mutual attraction increases over time; treasure every opportunity to open your hearts to each other.

CHAPTER 10

A New World Is Born

_When the Authentic Self in one person recognizes the Authentic Self
in another, a new world is born. We discover heaven on earth. And when we
experience the ecstasy and purity of this awakened human context, we know
that this is everything, that we have truly discovered that which is sacred._

ANDREW COHEN

The path of enduring love is the path of awakening together.
When the Authentic Self or soul of one person recognizes the soul of
another and finds there a deep resonance, both are freed into the
dance of life together. This bonding of souls where two become one
is timeless and supersedes all levels of human friendship. There is a
profound feeling that the soul has found its own true reflection and
a delightful acceptance that the heart has entered its home of trust,
acceptance and belonging. Truly a new world is born!

How many couples do you know who have achieved deep levels
of love and contentment in their lives? There are many couples who
have purposely set out to enrich themselves and each other and have
bonded in ways that make their partnership soul-satisfying and
indestructible. Once you meet them, you won't easily forget them.
Their faces radiate and their voices resonate with an attractive
energy that can only be described as mature love. You suspect that

they have discovered the secrets to keeping romance and passion alive. They have traveled the path of authentic living together, braved life's storms and embraced love's mysteries, and there is no turning back. The magic that flows between them titillates your curiosity and you wonder how they do it. Many of them have shared their transformative experiences with us; we share with you the markers and signposts they have left along the path of love's journey.

The journey of shared love is a journey into the heart that is infused with the energy of the soul. Just as the heart is central to the body so too is love the over-arching focus in committed relationship. A love-filled heart radiates love, compassion, tenderness, joy and an exuberance and delight for life. The heart that is open to giving and receiving love is at peace with itself, enjoys balance and wholeness and lives harmoniously with others. Cultivating a trusting, loving, open heart takes time and tender nurturing. Love can be fragile and vulnerable and quickly protects itself when hurt or rejected. With time, these walls of protection come down in the secure environment of love's tender nurturance and acceptance.

Remember that the best relationship is one in which your love for each other exceeds your need for each other.

HIS HOLINESS THE DALAI LAMA

Love cannot be contained within the boundaries of the heart; it expands its capacities as it searches for its own likeness. The heart and the soul are intimately linked. While the heart hungers for loving connection, the soul longs for its soul mate, or, as John O'Donohue so beautifully describes it, the 'anam cara' as chronicled in the ancient Celtic wisdom.

The soul mate relationship, that honest reflection of oneself in the soul of another, is the greatest gift imaginable and the flowering of all intimate connection. In its presence, the very best in us springs to life; the once tentative shoots of burgeoning love burst into full bloom with irresistible fragrance and undeniable beauty.

After many years of living and growing together, Mike and Joyce described their relationship this way. *Our passion stems from our real, caring, mutual love. It comes from our commitment, our understanding and the great love we share with each other. After attending one of Austin & Mary's lectures, we went home and recorded our new insights.*

Joyce wrote: *Don't wait for Mike to ignite the passion. You do it. Don't wait! You have the power to make this love a lifetime affair. So grateful for the honesty we share and the many ways we have grown together.*

Mike wrote: *Good lovers are made, not born. Passion is not just about sex; it's about the loving warmth we share together in our most private moments. It's amazing how much I have learned about myself and how my life has changed since I met you.*

Other experiences were expressed by a number of couples who have long, stable relationships. They built their successful relationship on tenderness and caring and constantly found new ways to show the depth of their love. True happiness, they believe, comes from remembering how special this precious person is in their life and the willingness to nurture the passion they share together. They realized that *waking up together*; growing in awareness about themselves and each other is *The Best Possible Wedding Gift* – the gift that just keeps on giving!

Still others shared how they stimulate and generate creativity in their marriages by being filled with wonder and awe about each other. They don't allow their relationships to become familiar or stale. They never want to let what was once so precious become ordinary. There is a sense of commitment, a promise to keep the sparkle in their relationships, to hold onto the romance by really noticing each other, being present and celebrating even the little things. It's about sensually tuning minds and hearts to each other and experiencing the magic all over again.

When each is willing to take responsibility for the success of the relationship, there is no further need for excuses. Meeting every situation with truth and honoring its reality frees them into the fullness of each moment. They inspire each other to always do their best, and offer love and support in achieving personal and relationship goals. At this level of consciousness, relationship takes on a whole new dimension.

Love withers with predictability;
its very essence is surprise and amazement.
To make love a prisoner of the
mundane is to take its passion and lose it forever.

LEO BUSCAGLIA

Living and Loving with Passion

Keep the passion alive! That's the secret to an amazing marriage. No one can give it to you. It's that indescribable something you have to want, really want. It's about waking up to the dormant possibilities for love and fanning them so they catch fire in you. This experience of passion is the secret to making your marriage extraordinary. It is this passion for life and love, this giving and sharing of your deepest self that makes your marriage sparkle. This desire must burn inside both of you. It's that depth of feeling that carries you through the difficult times and makes molehills out of mountains. A heart and soul ablaze with passion compel you to do what to some may seem impossible. Take no heed of the naysayers. The strength, beauty and power of marriage can be the most amazing way to journey through life. Passionate people can go where no others have gone.

Keeping the Magic Alive

Loving men and women who wholeheartedly invest themselves

in giving and receiving love make good marriages. The ability to create married happiness cannot be bought, rented or inherited. It has to be newly designed by each couple that commits to a shared life together. Passionate lovers can make blissful marriages whether their parents had an awesome or an awful relationship.

Some believe art imitates life, while others think life imitates art. We pondered that question as we stood before French painter Jean Auguste Cot's painting of *The Storm* at the Metropolitan Museum of Art in New York. The painting shows a young couple rushing to shelter from the dark gloomy weather. Young, innocent, but fully protective of each other, they screen themselves from the ravages of the storm with a simple swath of cloth. It's the imagery of the couple that is captivating. This nineteenth century painter stirs our imagination with his deft use of sensual pose; the arms of the lovers gently but firmly hold each other. One immediately supposes that their world of touch embraces the act of presence. Clearly the lovers move as one in a rhythm of intimacy. The painting conveys a feeling of aliveness, a deep sense of comfortable belonging, subtly expresses the language of touch, and reveals the shelter of warmth afforded by the intimacy of their togetherness.

The palette of color in any relationship can be vibrant, or dull. You choose how you wish to paint your own picture for your marriage. You have the canvas. You have the paintbrushes and the full assortment of colors. Together you've decided what you want your masterpiece to be. How much tone and texture, shade and subtlety have you added? Is it rich and vibrant, or gray and dull? It's never too late to add color and beauty to the canvas of your shared lives. Let all who observe your canvas be inspired by the richness and intensity, the flow and subtle blend of nature's glorious hues. The ongoing journey is about deciding together how grand and beautiful, rich and wondrous your togetherness can be and how willing you are to explore the nature and depth of love's ancient call to your souls.

The call of your soul is to self-actualization. Abraham Maslow hypothesizes that we reach the ultimate stage of human development when we meet our need for food, shelter, family, health, education, social integration and a sense of accomplishment intellectually, socially and materially. He went on to define this experience of well-being as spiritual (the intensity of the emotional and intellectual energy of your soul). To the degree that we are *actualized* we will experience creativity, playfulness, joy and a sense of purpose in our life. Life's highest purpose is that of becoming authentic, fully realized, human beings.

The energy that attracted your souls to each other continues to unfold in your awareness as you advance daily into that awakened level of purposeful living described by Maslow. Self-realization, honesty and the willingness to embrace reality constitute the driving commitments that cause you to leave behind your old emotional states of fear, anxiety and confusion. The call to your soul is to listen less to the internal chatter of the ego, to let go of self-centered preoccupation, and thus free yourself to participate more fully in your relationship with life and everyone in it.

Life in our universe is all about relationship. Albert Einstein tells us that *thinking of our self as separate from the rest is a 'kind of optical delusion of one's consciousness.'* He says we *must free ourselves from this prison of delusion by widening our circle of love to embrace all living creatures and the whole of nature in its beauty.* The universe in its wisdom brings us a soul mate so we can create a new sense of self and thereby transform our very nature. Relationship fully embraced and authentically lived is the bearer of gifts. Inside the gift boxes you will discover your life lessons delivered in a way that causes no more pain. The truth about yourself and your purpose unfolds in conscious awareness and ushers in a new level of living filled with grace.

The French poet, Guillaume Apollinaire voiced this calling to the soul:

> *Come to the edge, he said.*
> *They said: We are afraid.*
> *Come to the edge, he said.*
> *They came.*
> *He pushed them…and they flew.*

The Path of Awakening Together

The call to awakening, to fly beyond anything we currently know, opens us to the newness of ourselves. This newness is often birthed in risk and faltering steps. It is in the unexplored territory of 'not knowing' that we discover the richest treasures. This courageous blending of hearts and souls in intimate relationship provides the key to unraveling the mystery of our deepest self. Lovers, whose hearts have found shelter and compassion in each other, discover a mysterious quality of enchantment that infuses their lives. Together they enter into the Mysterium – that magical, invisible soul place where love awakens in them those longings and threads of connections. It is the awakening heart that yearns for belonging, life, love, sharing, togetherness and oneness. Only in this sacred space, where two friends become one soul (Euripides, the Greek dramatist's description of soul mates), can they experience the breadth and depth, the beauty and wonder of love's most precious gifts. These sensations of joy and delight are reserved for those who willingly risk spreading their wings so they can rendezvous in the pleasant warmth of their connected souls and be forever filled with the rich blessing of enduring love.

As you walk the path of relationship together, you will recognize some markers and milestones. When you have the courage to look deep within yourself, confront your false self and the stories it creates to defend and justify itself, you find a reservoir of truth and a growing awareness of your own power and beauty. You will be able to separate what is real from what is illusion. The insights that come into your field of awareness will usher in a new sense of peace and a heightened level of fulfillment. You will recognize how life is lived from the inside out. Never again will you feel inclined to project your story on your partner. As you continue to grow spiritually, you will have a new sense of appreciation for everyone and everything around you. Your life will become a continual flow of welcome life-learning events that come with ease and grace.

Markers and Milestones

1. *You will feel loved.* You feel a new sense of belonging as you allow yourself to feel comfortable in the shelter of your lover's heart. Your love grows because you no longer expect your lover to be as you want him or her to be. A 'new you' is beginning to emerge.

2. *You will find balance and harmony in your shared love.* You are growing in your understanding that your lover is a reflection of yourself. You now take ownership of your past emotional experiences and are willing to see yourself as you really are. No longer do you blame people or events for the unhappiness in your life. You realize that your inner thoughts and dialogue are the director and producer of your life events and that you can change them at will.

3. *You will develop your own couple style.* You are expressing your own unique way of being in relationship. Together you are deciding what has value to you and how you want to evolve your shared lives. Dreams for your future are shaped and honed in the sanctuary of your togetherness and your focus is clearer.

4. *You will feel nurtured.* You have a matured sense of how to satisfy each other; care for each other's needs and recognize gender preferences. The old unconscious behaviors are replaced with growthful ones; you encourage rather than criticize, take responsibility rather than blame the other, assist rather than complain, exercise control rather than anger. Differences are resolved with compassion and understanding.

5. *You will feel happy and content.* You are both becoming fluent in the language of love. You listen with your heart and are present to each other. Consultation on matters concerning your life and love is easy and effortless. The honesty and truth discovered in your self-realization frees you from the past; the real beauty of your souls shines through your lives.

6. *You will feel relaxed and healthy.* Through honest soul-searching you now understand what triggers stress reactions, and have adopted your own techniques/practices for managing them. Roles and responsibilities are lovingly performed as your personal contribution to the peaceful, relaxed environment of your marriage and home. You relish healthy choices mentally, emotionally and physically.

7. *You will feel financially stable.* You enjoy peace of mind because you are putting your life and your marriage on the road to

financial security. You establish mutually agreeable priorities for spending and saving. Because you are in control of your finances, all stress concerning money has receded from your relationship.

8. *You will feel sexually satisfied with your partner.* Your private intimate time is a very important priority in your life. You continue to find each other attractive, desirable and sensual. Deep feelings are easily communicated through loving gestures and rituals of affection. You delightfully indulge in erotic pleasure and mutual tenderness.

9. *You will feel passionate about life.* You experience a deep feeling of contentment and a passion for the exhilarating joy of life. Unbounded, you have a sense that you can face anything together with courage and style. The threads of your multiple experiences (triumphs and tragedies) weave themselves into a magnificent tapestry that is indestructible. Outsiders observe a sparkle and a glow about you that can only be forged in the intimacy of shared lives and committed hearts.

10. *You will experience real happiness.* You no longer yearn for anything, content with your achievements on the intellectual, social and material levels. You are living authentic lives, feel spiritually fulfilled, creative and deeply bonded. This is self-actualization. Friends, family and colleagues ponder the strength

and power of your togetherness. You are fulfilling your original purpose to evolve as human beings. The sharing of your deepest selves and the constant flow of newness that this births in your souls is the true soul mate relationship realized.

Abélard and Héloïse, the renowned lovers, share their parting thoughts on the depth of their love.

Abélard: *"In our intense encounters, we explored every facet of love; we exhausted all of the subtleties that passion can imagine."*

Héloïse: *"These sensual pleasures that we relished together were so delightful that I love to revisit them, and never want to erase their sweet memory."*

The mystery of shared love has its own power and presence. When a couple wakes up together they move out of the concealed place that once captured their hearts into the brightness of a breaking dawn. A new world is born. In the light of love, fear gives way to confidence; undisclosed secrets become intimate sharings; the previously shriveled heart beats with grace and beauty. In the light of awakened passion, souls are freed into the rhythm and dance of Life.

SELECTED BIBLIOGRAPHY

Abélard et Héloïse. *Abélard et Héloïse Correspondence*. Translated and compiled by Paul Zumthor. Paris: Union Generale d'Editions, 1979.

Andrews, Frank. *The Art and Practice of Loving*. LA: Jeremy P Tarcher Inc. 1991.

Berne, Eric. *Games People Play, The Psychology of Human Relationships*. New York: Grove Press, 1964.

Berne, Eric. *What Do You Say After You Say Hello?* New York: Grove Press, 1972.

Borysenko, Joan. *Guilt Is the Teacher, Love is the Lesson*. New York: Warner Books 1990.

Borysenko, Joan. *Minding the Body, Mending the Mind*. New York: Bantam Books, 1988.

Buscaglia, Leo. *Loving Each Other: The Challenge of Human Relationships*. New York: Fawcett, 1984.

Buscaglia, Leo. *Love*: New York: Fawcett Crest 1985.

Buzan, Tony. *The Power of Spiritual Intelligence: 10 Ways to Tap into Your Spiritual Genius*. London: Thorsons, 2001.

Campbell, Susan M. *The Couples Journey: Intimacy as a Path to Wholeness*. San Luis Obispo, CA: Impact Publishers, 1984.

Capacchione, Lucia. *Visioning: Ten Steps to Designing the Life of Your Dreams*. New York: Jeremy P. Tarcher/Putnam, 2000.

Casarjian, Robin. *Forgiveness: A Bold Choice for a Peaceful Heart*. New York: Bantam Books, 1992.

Chilton, David. *The Wealthy Barber: The Common Sense Guide to Successful Financial Planning*. Toronto: Stoddart Publishing Co., 1989.

Chopra, Deepak. *Unconditional Life: Mastering the Forces That Shape Personal Reality*. New York: Bantam Books, 1991.

Clinebell, Howard J. & Charlotte H. *The Intimate Marriage*. New York: Harper & Row, 1970.

Cohen, Andrew. *Living Enlightenment: a call for evolution beyond ego*. Lennox, Mass. Moksha Press, 2002.

Dyer, Wayne. *Your Sacred Self: Making the Decision to Be Free*. New York: Harper Collins, 1995.

Finley, Guy. *The Secret of Letting Go*. St Paul, MN: Llewellyn Publications, 1994.

Finley, Guy. *Apprentice of the Heart: Lessons in Life Only Love Can Teach*. Ashland, Oregon: White Cloud Press, 2004.

Fromm, Erich. *The Art of Loving*. New York: Harper & Row, 1956.

Gawain, Shakti. *The Path of Transformation: How Healing Ourselves Can Change The World*. CA: Nataraj Publishing, 1993.

Glasser, William. *Reality Therapy*. New York: Harper and Row, 1965.

Glasser, William, and Carleen Glasser. *Getting Together and Staying Together: Solving the Mystery of Marriage*. New York: Harper Collins, 2000.

Goddard, Neville. *The Magic of Imagination*. CA: Canterbury House, 1992.

Goleman, Daniel. *Emotional Intelligence: Why it can matter more than IQ*. New York: Bantam Books, 1995.

Gray, John. *Men, Woman and Relationships: Making Peace with the Opposite Sex*. Hillsboro, Oregon: Beyond Words Publishing, 1993.

Harley, Willard F. Jr. *His Needs Her Needs: Building An Affair-proof Marriage*. Grand Rapids, Mi: Fleming H. Revell, 1986.

Helmstetter, Shad. *What to Say When You Talk to Yourself: Powerful New Techniques to Program Your Potential for Success*. New York: Simon & Schuster, 1982.

Hendricks, Gay and Kathleen. *Conscious Loving: The Journey to Co-Commitment*. New York: Bantam Books, 1992.

Hendrix, Harville. *Getting The Love You Want: A Guide For Couples*. New York: Harper and Row, 1990.

Howard, Vernon. *Pathways to Perfect Living*. New York: Stein and Day, 1985.

James, Muriel, and Dorothy Jongeward. *Born to Win: Transactional Analysis with Gestalt Experiments*. Reading, Mass.: Addison-Wesley, 1971.

Jeffers, Susan. *Feel The Fear and Do It Anyway*. New York: Fawcett Columbine, 1987.

Johnson, Robert. *We: Understanding the Psychology of Romantic Love*. New York: Harper & Row, 1985.

Kabat-Zinn, Jon. *Full Catastrophe Living*. New York: Delacorte Press, 1990.

Katie, Byron, with Stephen Mitchell. *Loving What Is: Four Questions That Can Change Your Life*. New York: Three Rivers Press, 2002.

Kaufman, Barry Neil. *To Love Is To Be Happy With*. New York: Ballentine Books, 1983.

Kiyosaki, Robert T. *Rich Dad, Poor Dad*. New York: Warner Books, 2000.

Larson, Christian D. *The Ideal Made Real*. CA: Newcastle Publishing, 1995.

Lerner, Michael. *Spirit Matters: Global Healing and the Wisdom of the Soul*. VA: Hampton Roads Publishing Co. Inc., 2000.

Lesser, Elizabeth. *The New American Spirituality: A Seeker's Guide*. New York: Random House, 1999.

Lepp, Ignace. *The Psychology of Loving*. Translated by Bernard B. Gilligan. Dublin: Helicon Limited, 1964.

Levine, Stephen. *A Gradual Awakening*. New York: Doubleday (Anchor Books), 1979.

Luhes, Janet. *Simple Loving: A Path to Deeper, More Sustainable Relationships*. New York: Penguin Group, 2000.

Mace, David R. *Close Companions: The Marriage Enrichment Handbook*. New York: The Continuum Publishing Company, 1987.

Maslow, Abraham. *Towards a Psychology of Being* (2d ed) New York: Van Nostrand, Reinhold, 1968.

Maslow, Abraham. *The Further Reaches of Human Nature*. New York: Viking, 1975.

May, Rollo. *Love and Will*. New York: W. W. Norton, 1969.

Moore, Thomas. *Soul Mates: Honoring the Mysteries of Love and Relationship*. New York: Harper Collins, 1994.

Moschetta, Evelyn & Paul. *The Marriage Spirit: Finding the Passion and Joy of Soul Centered Love*. New York: Simon & Schuster, 1998.

O'Donohue, John. *Anam Cara: A Book of Celtic Wisdom*. New York: Harper Collins, 1997.

Orman, Suze. *The 9 Steps to Financial Freedom: Practical & Spiritual Steps So You Can Stop Worrying*. New York: Crown Publishers, 1997.

Ouspensky, P. D. *The Psychology of Man's Possible Evolution*. New York: Vintage Books, 1974.

Page, Susan. *How One of You Can Bring the Two of You Together*. New York: Broadway Books, 1997.

Pearsall, Paul. *The Ten Laws of Lasting Love*. New York: Avon Books, 1993.

Pernoud, Regine. *Héloïse et Abélard*. Paris: Albin Michel, 1970.

Powell, John. *Why Am I Afraid to Love?* Texas: Argus Communications, 1982.

Reeves, Paula M. *Heart Sense: Unlocking Your Highest Purpose and Deepest Desires*. Boston: Conari Press, 2003.

Rogers, Carl. *Client Centered Therapy*. Boston: Houghton Mifflin, 1951.

Rohn, Jim. *Seven Strategies for Wealth and Happiness*. Rocklin, CA: Prima Publishing, 1986.

Ruiz, Don Miguel. *The Four Agreements: A Toltec Wisdom Book*. San Rafael, CA: Amber-Allen Publishing, 1997.

Ruiz, Don Miguel. *The Mastery of Love: A Toltec Wisdom Book*. San Rafael, CA: Amber-Allen Publishing, 1999.

Schnarch, David. *The Passionate Marriage: Keeping Love and Intimacy Alive in Committed Relationships*. New York: Henry Holt & Co., 1997.

Sellner, Judith A. and James G. Sellner. *Loving For Life: Your Self-help Guide to a Successful, Intimate Relationship*. North Vancouver, B.C.: Self-Counsel Press, 1991.

Teilhard de Chardin, Pierre. *The Phenomenon of Man*. New York: Harper and Row, 1959.

Walsch, Neale Donald. *The New Revelations: A Conversation with God*. New York: Atria Books, 2002.

Walters, J. Donald. *Expansive Marriage: A Way to Self-Realization*. Nevada City, CA: Crystal Clarity, 1995.

Wilber, Ken. *The Spectrum of Consciousness*. Wheaton, Ill: The Theosophical Publishing House, 1989.

Williamson, Marianne. *A Return to Love: Reflections on the Principles of A Course in Miracles*. New York: HarperCollins, 1992.

Williamson, Marianne. *Enchanted Love: The Mystical Power of Intimate Relationships*. New York: Simon & Schuster, 1999.

Wolf, Sharyn. *How To Stay Lovers for Life: Discover a Marriage Counselor's Tricks of the Trade*. New York: Penguin Books, 1997.

Wolinsky, Stephen. *Trances People Live: Healing Approaches In Quantum Psychology*. CT: The Brambles Company, 1991.

Zukav, Gary. *The Seat of the Soul*. New York: Simon & Schuster (Firestone) 1989.

If you would like to learn more about the Hennessey's Relationship Mentoring or about their weekly lectures on authentic living, contact them at: **thehennesseys@shaw.ca**

Professional speakers, they are available for keynote presentations to groups and organizations.

ISBN 141203777-8